THE FEAST OF CHRISTMAS

Paul Levy was born in Kentucky in 1941 and educated at the universities of Chicago, London, Harvard and Oxford. A lapsed academic, he has for many years been both Lytton Strachey's co-literary executor and, until 1992, the Food and Wine Editor of the *Observer*. He writes frequently for the *Wall Street Journal* on general cultural matters and lives in a 17th-century Oxfordshire farmhouse with his wife, two daughters and an awful lot of cats.

Paul Levy is also the author or editor of: Lytton Strachey: The Really Interesting Question and Other Papers (Ed.); Moore: G. E. Moore and the Cambridge Apostles; The Shorter Strachey (Ed. with Michael Holroyd); The Official Foodie Handbook (with Ann Barr); Out to Lunch; and Finger Lickin' Good: A Kentucky Childhood

The Feast of Christmas

Paul Levy

with photographs by Robin Broadbent

Kyle Cathie Limited

For Tatyana and Georgia

First published in Great Britain by
Kyle Cathie Limited
3 Vincent Square London SW1P 2LX

Copyright © 1992 by Paul Levy
Copyright © 1992 in the food
photographs by Robin Broadbent

ISBN hardcover 1 85626 070 4
paperback 1 85626 071 2

A CIP catalogue record for this book is
available from the British Library

Photoset by Rowland Phototypesetting
Ltd, Bury St Edmunds, Suffolk
Printed in Great Britain by
Butler and Tanner Ltd,
Frome and London

Contents

Acknowledgements

For their practical help with this book the author wishes to thank the following: Edward Behr, Frances and Tom Bissell, Maggie Black, Raymond and Koti Cottrell, Kyle Cathie, Alan and Jane Davidson, Georgina Denison, Fiona Fairbairn, the late M. F. K. Fisher, Chris Goddard, Steve Hatt, Julia Hodgkin, Ken Hom, Hazel Horrobin, Philip and Mary Hyman, Joy Larkcom, Jenny Lo, Patricia Lousada, Penelope Marcus, John Munson, John Noble, Richard Olney, Camellia Panjabi, Namita Panjabi, Claudia Roden, Dennis Severs, Hilary Spurling, Anne Willan and Marc Cherniavsky, Hilary Bird for the index and Mark Walford.

Credits

Food for photography prepared by Mary Cadogan, styling by Penny Markham. Chicken from Bennett's Farm, Dorking, Surrey (0306 711598), cheese from Neal's Yard Dairy, ham from Dukeshill Ham Company, Bridgnorth, Shropshire (0704 635519), fish from Steve Hatt, Essex Road, London N1 (071 226 3963). The following supplied food for the cover shot: W. Bainborough Ltd and Jeroboams of Elizabeth Street, London SW1.

Picture acknowledgements

The Author and Publishers wish to thank the following for permission to use illustrations:

Bridgeman Art Library pages 15, 23, 25, 42, 58, 85, 89, 90, 144; Windsor Castle, Royal Library, © 1992 Her Majesty the Queen page 19; Jacqui Hurst pages 35, 39, 114, 116; Sonia Halliday and Laura Lustington page 24; Illustrated London News pages 24, 83; Mary Evans Picture Library pages 78, 111, 177; Harrods Ltd Company Archives page 95; the Stilton Cheese Makers' Association and Osborne Publicity Services Ltd pages 143, 144, 145; and Appleby's of Hawkstone page 148.

The television series, **The Feast of Christmas**, is a Malone Gill Production for Channel 4, produced by Georgina Dennison and directed by Chris Goddard.

Introduction

Once a year our dismal diet disappears, and the gloom of national culinary mediocrity lifts. (Americans have the bonus of a twice-a-year food high, thanks to Thanksgiving.) For the rest of the year, we may merely eat, snack, graze or nosh; but at Christmas we feast.

Poor old Anglo-Saxons. We have to get ourselves in a special frame of mind to eat better than we usually do. We have to decorate our houses and buy presents for our children, just to get us in the mood. How unlike the run of mankind we are in this respect. I have known students in Shanghai who were actually *hungry* (a condition little known in the junk-food overfed West) and who, when invited to a dinner at a restaurant they could never afford, and offered food of a quantity and quality they may seldom or never have seen, showed a critical appreciation of what was set before them. They did not wolf down the delicate steamed fish with its slivers of ginger and garlic, though that was probably the method usually employed to get through their twice-daily ration of half a pound of gritty boiled rice with a couple of tablespoons of vegetables and a scrap of fatty pork. These students, who had latched on to our party to practise their English, and not in the hope of getting a square meal, showed by their demeanour, their table manners and the fashion in which they savoured every bite, slowly and reflectively, that though they may have been almost starving, they knew how to feast.

The same respectful, reflective attitude towards food exists, still, in most European countries: the meanest peasant, who may subsist, involuntarily, on a diet of grains and vegetables, still knows how to feast. This grace before meals, this attitude that allows food to be savoured (or despised if it is not up to standard) is a gift given by the culture; a gift transmitted by parents and grandparents, which is the direct result of the closeness of their association with the soil. Of course this gift is no blessing if the soil has let them down, if the crops have been poor and nature has been mean. But when there is food on the table (and, usually, wine in the glass), the person with the talent for feasting is capable of having an experience of enjoyment, of the enhancing of life, that is all but denied to us who get our food shrink-wrapped from a stripbulb-lighted supermarket.

Still, once a year we are given a glimpse of what food can mean to man. Instinctively we know the importance of feasting. Indeed, we feel at Christmas that it is everyone's *right* to feast. It is not only in hospitals, factory canteens and army messes that a special effort is made at Christmas; even those who are nourished only by soup kitchens, and prisoners in their jails, are given better food at this time of year.

What is it that distinguishes the attitude of the feaster from that of the ordinary eater? In what frame of mind do we approach the feast? First, of course, there is the anticipation of sensory pleasure — we expect to enjoy ourselves more than usual (and some to enjoy themselves more than enough; it is idle to deny that for some people the pleasure of the feast includes licensed gluttony). Secondly, there is the prospect of social pleasure, of at least a short time of comradeship and good fellowship, even if it is limited to a few hours around a table.

But thirdly, and this may be startling if you have never thought about it before, there is an intellectual reward. The ancients knew this: after all, there was a bite to eat served with the wine at Plato's Symposium. The pleasures of the table are enhanced by reflecting on them (despite the horrid upper-class English ban on discussing the food at table, which lasted well into the 1960s). Curiosity about what we put in our mouths is a very good thing, and a pleasurable cast of mind. Why is this turkey so moist, when another cook's version of this bird is a dry and sorry thing? Where did the turkey originate? How did it get its name? Why do we eat it at Christmas?

At the feast, everyone is a critic.

If we have enough food, we take it for granted. It is only when there is too little, or more than enough, that we reflect about what we chew and swallow. Food is surrounded by myths, some of which are nonsense (such as that 'toadstools' are poisonous, but mushrooms are delicious; that you can tell one from the other by peeling them, or cutting them with a silver knife). Each item of food has its own history (what was Italian food like before Columbus discovered the Americas and tomatoes, or Indian food before Portuguese travellers brought them chillies?). Food has glamour (why do we prize caviar, when the sailor, tasting it for the first time, said 'Hello, this jam tastes like fish'?). We are obsessed by food (there are chocoholics who can't get enough of it, and anorexics for whom any amount is too much). There are dangers in some foods (I once contracted salmonella from an egg, and the Japanese devotees of *fugu*, poisonous blow-fish, risk death with each bite). Food is surrounded by taboos (Muslims and Jews won't eat pork, many Americans shun animal fat).

Even the most ordinary pedestrian, everyday meal reveals, when reflected upon, curious facts of history, science and human relations. One of the most fascinating books of recent years was written by a Canadian classicist who, peeling and chopping onions for a familiar Elizabeth David recipe, suddenly stopped and asked herself why onions stung her eyes, why some were hard to peel and others easy, why some were red and some yellow or white. Where did they come from? Was it true that onions were the main food of the Egyptian workmen who built the pyramids? How do onions figure in folk medicine? Margaret Visser visited the library the next day, and began the research that culminated in *Much Depends on Dinner*, in whose 300-odd pages she analyses every aspect of a representative North American meal. History – and not just the history of food – will never be the same. She has breathed intellectual life, and new and exciting savours, into an activity most of us do three times a day.

I hope to do something like that for our annual midwinter binge, to inspect the feast course by course, and follow my nose, taste buds and curiosity wherever they take me. The investigation will take me to some peculiar places because my own family's Christmas menu is eclectic, and in what follows I examine the Christmas feast that my family and friends have held for several years. Though we basically eat the sort of meal that is customary in English-speaking countries, our family celebrations were formerly held in France, and as a result we have acquired some Frenchified ways.

Moreover, I am Jewish by birth. Though not observant, I have a strong Jewish cultural strain – in my being and in what anthropologists uncharmingly call 'foodways'. Though born in America – another important strand in explaining the food I put on our table – I live with my family in Britain; and Britain now has a culture, especially as regards food, made up of several ethnic and national traditions. We – all of us – are now as likely to go out for an Indian or Chinese meal as for fish and chips. This is as true for those living in small towns as for those living in cities. Our own Christmas turkey, as you will see from the following pages, is just as likely to be cooked with soy sauce and star anise, or to be studded with black truffles, as to be plainly roasted and stuffed with sage, onion and breadcrumbs.

This book proceeds, as does the television series it accompanies, course by course.

Paul Levy
OXFORD
JUNE 1992

9

CHAPTER ONE

The case for Christmas

Every family has its own, personal Christmas traditions. Ours involve elaborate planning and – to tell the truth – prolonging and emphasising as much as possible the pleasurable anticipation of the feast. We are seldom fewer than 18 at table for the Christmas meal, which has evolved into a stately chorus line, choreographed by my wife and me with the help of the principal dancers, who include some well-known professional cookery writers, and supported by the teamwork of the rest of the guests. At noon we gather in front of the fire in the drawing room and drink champagne while the children open their presents. Guests wander in through the front door of our 17th-century Oxfordshire farmhouse from noon until we sit down to eat at four.

Anyone who comes before four is either co-opted for kitchen duty, or follows my wife, Penny, on a long and strenuous walk down into the Combe Valley. The younger men are enlisted to move the furniture: the kitchen deal tables are put end to end, and the lower raised on four bricks that are stored in the pantry. The white damask tablecloths have been ironed with sugar. The fruit, flowers and foliage are arranged on the table. The menu cards, made by my younger daughter Georgia, are put out as the table is laid with all the cutlery and glasses we can muster.

The kitchen, a converted milking parlour and dairy, is about forty feet long. The table is set up at one end, while the cooks gather around the Aga at the other end. On the table side, the oyster-openers are at work, while other guest-workers are in the garden picking the sprouts, salad and herbs. Frances Bissell, *The Times* cook, is supervising the turkey, while Claudia Roden, the leading authority on Middle Eastern food, leads her team down to the cellar to collect the apples to go with the truffled *boudin blanc*. Somehow, every year, as if by magic, we are ready to crowd around the table precisely at four. Penny has done the seating plan, which is tricky, as the chief cooks have to be able to get to the Aga.

Though we introduce some (usually subtle) variations each time, the menu is basically fixed. Champagne with Middle Eastern nibbles prepared by Claudia. Then, at table, oysters (raw, plus cooked for the squeamish) with an alternative of smoked salmon. *Boudin blanc* with apples. Sometimes a large whole fish, or a terrine of scallops and turkey. The bird, formerly goose or pheasant, but now turkey (since the discovery of turkey-farmer John Munson's old-fashioned birds), is treated a little differently each year. One year it was quickly roasted, unstuffed, and carved so rapidly you could scarcely follow his

movement by the celebrated chef Raymond Blanc, who then proceeded to reconstruct it, and brought it to the table still hot. Another year the entire meal was cooked single-handedly by Ken Hom, the Chinese-American cookery teacher and writer, who was too tired to carve the turkey so he lifted the breasts and sliced them into thick, succulent steaks. One year someone gave me a truffle. We shaved it thinly and placed the slices under the skin, thus producing the famous dish of turkey *en demi-deuil* – in half-mourning, because of the black of the truffles.

Frances hates Brussels sprouts, so Anton Mosimann taught me a trick to win her around to them: we shred them finely, and stir-fry them in the wok with garlic and ginger. Next we always have a green salad; we cultivate the garden with an eye to having salad all year round. The cheese is always Colston Bassett stilton (not the same since the farmers who make up the Colston Bassett cooperative took fright in the listeria scare of 1988 and went over to pasteurisation, but still the best stilton there is), a medium-sized truckle of Mr Keen's cheddar, aged 18–24 months, and a small truckle of Mrs Appleby's cheshire. Christmas pudding comes from Anton Mosimann and is served flaming with the lights out (it is always dark outside by this stage of the meal), followed by a huge Moroccan filo pastry 'snake', filled with almond paste scented with rosewater and orange-blossom water, made in advance by Claudia.

At this point we pull the crackers, put on our funny hats and read the bad jokes to each other. Chocolates, dried fruits and cobnuts from the garden are on the table with the port. And anyone with the energy to do it makes the coffee.

We try each year to drink some of the same wines as the year before, and pretend that we are assessing the vintage. In fact, we think carefully about the wines for the meal, and plan as far in advance as possible. There's always plenty of champagne, and we usually have an interesting still white wine, a claret and either a burgundy or a wine from the south of France.

We are positively burdened with Christmas traditions; we have collective nostalgia. Though the guest list changes a little every year, the hard core is unchanging. All of us are interested in food and wine, and there's always a mother-in-law and an honorary aunt or two, plus some of our children's godparents; the rest of us are the gastronomic waifs and strays, some without children, some whose children have grown up and left home – though a surprising number of this last category end up around this same table every year.

THE LEVY FAMILY CHRISTMAS REALLY BEGINS WHEN we go out to the orchard and dig up the Christmas tree from its parking space, where we put it each January 6, and lug it into the house; then we cut the holly from one of our old trees. Though the Romans used to decorate trees at this time of year, and even bring them into the house, the Christmas tree itself was introduced, both to England and America, by German immigrants in the 1830s and 1840s. As the British royal family were of German background, Christmas trees were introduced in the reigns of both George III and William IV, though of course they really caught on when Victoria and Albert erected their tree at Windsor in 1840. (The famous scene of Victoria and Albert and the royal family by their

Christmas tree appeared in the *Illustrated London News* in 1848.)

Our ritual continues with the search in the glory hole for the wicker hamper with the family decorations, and we go through the usual process of cursing on finding that the fairylights are fused because one tiny bulb isn't working. We painstakingly search for the culprit light, and we resist the usual demands of the children to make the tree as gaudy as possible. We remark on what a pity it is that all this work must be undone in 12 days' time, and explain to the children the superstitions connected with leaving the greenery up beyond Twelfth Night.

Oddly enough, though, the traditions of decorating the house with evergreens and lights and exchanging gifts did not come from the northern European Yule tradition, but from the southern European midwinter festivals of the later Roman Empire, particularly Saturnalia, which started on December 17. Saturnalia was a feast presided over by a Master of the Revels, sometimes the Lord of Misrule. Everything was turned upside down: masters waited on their servants (as still happens in the messes of the British Army on Christmas Day); gambling and drunkenness, forbidden during the rest of the year, were encouraged; children cheeked their parents; and there was licence even in matters of dress. Men wore animal skins or dressed as women, and women dressed as men.

If that puts you in mind of the Christmas pantomime, that's precisely where its cross-dressing traditions have come from. Our local pantomime, in the town of Chipping Norton, takes place every season in a tiny theatre converted from a chapel. Many of the same people attend every year, and there is a cosy feeling because many of the audience are acquainted with the actors as well as each other. The children are extremely well rehearsed, and know when to hiss and boo, and at what point the sweets will be thrown from the stage. Perhaps the pantomime itself will involve making a particularly butch male member of the audience come on to the stage and put on a frock, as it did the year before last.

Back at home as we wrap the presents we think about gift-giving and the other winter festivals. The Jewish Hanukkah is 'the feast of lights', commemorating the Maccabees' successful recovery of the temple, when one day's supply of oil miraculously lasted for eight days. Children get presents, sometimes on each of the eight days, a candle is lit each night; and there are special foods – latkes, particularly (see page 118 for recipe). Hindu Dewali is also a festival of light, and for the two weeks before it people exchange gifts of sweetmeats – the sweet shops are absolutely full of goods during the period.

Our own customs come from gift-giving at Kalends, the Roman New Year, a tradition still maintained by the French and, until this very generation, by the Scots, who have only recently begun to celebrate Christmas as well as Hogmanay, for Scotsman John Knox's condemnation of Christmas had much more effect than the dislike of it expressed by Cromwell and the English Puritans.

The real key to Christmas, though, is nostalgia. Even the children worry that the coming Christmas will not be as good as past ones, and are very conservative about, for example, having the red lacquer apples on the tree in the same places as last year, and having turkey rather than ham or beef for the main Christmas meal. Psychologists will tell us that family traditions continue because all parents consciously seek to preserve bits of their own past, of their own childhood.

My own family's Christmas traditions were fairly thin on the ground. The Levys of Lexington, Kentucky, the small town in the southern states of America where I was born, were the children of Russian Jewish immigrants, and at first they tolerated Christmas rather than celebrated it. But by the time I was 12 they had given in to the customs of the majority of the neighbours, at least in the matter of Christmas presents. I owe my present indifference to chocolates to the Christmas when a Roman Catholic step-aunt gave my brother and me each a two-pound box of chocolates. I had eaten most of them by the time the grown-ups woke up on Christmas Day, and have never wanted to repeat the experience. So, like the Victorians, I entertain a nostalgia for a Christmas that never really was. The difference is that the Victorians (mis)placed their ideal Christmas in the 18th century, probably the one era in modern British history when Christmas was least celebrated.

To see why that was so, we must just look very briefly at the history of Christmas. Saturnalia, the direct ancestor of Christmas, was celebrated, following Julius Caesar's reform of the calendar, on December 17. Augustus decreed that the 17th should be sacred to Saturn and the 18th to Ops, Saturn's wife. From then on these two days were celebrated as Saturnalia, though the holidays were later extended by several days. The Romans identified Saturn with the Greek Cronus (or Kronos), the agricultural god of harvests. Though not much is known about his cults (he may well have been the divinity of a pre-Hellenic people), his reign was regarded as a Golden Age. In the Roman version, Saturn fled to Italy after the fall of the Titans and settled on the Capitoline Hill. He civilised the people and taught them the skills of farming. In celebration of his mission to Rome gifts were exchanged, schools and courts were closed, war was forbidden and slaves and masters ate at the same table. This celebration, called the Saturnalia, was the origin of the topsy-turvy tradition. The traditions lingered on into the 19th century. In 1856, Frederick Law Olmstead, the remarkable historian of American slavery, said he had noticed in his travels in the Confederacy that 'from Christmas to New Year's Day, most of the slaves, except house servants, enjoy a freedom from labour; and Christmas is especially holiday, or Saturnalia, with them'. It is curious to reflect that the upside-down aspects of Christmas celebrations from the Middle Ages to our own day all derive from this noble Roman seasonal respite from slavery. At the winter solstice we laugh, we gamble, we even drink a little too much, perhaps because we share this folk memory of a Golden Age.

The early church did not celebrate the birth of Jesus – indeed, not much notice was taken of anybody's birthday, as its celebration was largely a pagan practice. In any case, there wasn't much point in marking the Incarnation as early Christians expected the Second Coming to happen in their own time. Thus it wasn't until the 4th century that the Bishop of Rome, Julius I, declared Christmas a feast. Naturally enough, when it came to setting the date the Church, as eager to keep its own members from lapsing as to

CHAPTER TWO

Let the feast begin

Is there a typical first course for Christmas lunch or dinner? In Paris, the answer would be *oui*: oysters, smoked salmon or foie gras; and many French families will lash out on one – or all three – of these luxuries for at least one of the *réveillons*. (Tradition is on their side: 'Oysters are the usual opening to a winter breakfast . . . indeed they are almost indispensable', pronounced the *Almanach des Gourmands* in 1803.) The same is increasingly true in Britain. And why not? After all, Scottish smoked salmon is certainly the best in the whole world, and I would make the same claim for English native oysters, if only they were more easily available for people to test whether I'm correct or not.

Historically, though, oysters have the strongest claim on our attention. Well into the present century they were the normal first course for the Christmas feast in Britain and America, as in France. Now, as the farming of oysters brings down their price, they are once again taking their place on the English-speaking Christmas table. In a way, they never lost that place in America, though they were often cooked, especially in the southern states, and they will appear in this form in a later course in this book.

In *North Atlantic Seafood*, the most authoritative book on the subject, Alan Davidson reckons that America has more recipes for cooked oysters than do the French or British because of the relative abundance of the bivalves on that side of the Atlantic. It is true that the cheaper oysters become, the more frequently they are cooked or even used as flavouring than eaten raw. In our own day the success of *ostréiculture* in driving prices down led those chefs connected with the *nouvelle cuisine* to derive ever more exquisite ways to cook oysters. In fact, all the cooking an oyster needs is to warm it through until its edges curl just a little (and then they can be eaten with impunity, even by people like my wife who has acquired a sort of 'allergy' to oysters from having once eaten a bad one). Or you can wrap them in blanched lettuce or spinach leaves and poach them for seconds in their own liquor plus a little cream, before replacing them in their shells and napping them with a reduction of the cooking liquid.

This is a counsel of *luxe*, for times when good things get less scarce than they have formerly been. But John Munson, who farms turkeys near Colchester, told me he can remember his grandmother adding oysters to steak and kidney pie not so much for their flavour as to increase the bulk, because they were so much cheaper than beef. This was borne out by Dickens in *Pickwick Papers*, when Sam Weller says 'It's a wery remarkable circumstance, sir, that poverty and oysters always seem to go together.'

Dickens thought oysters intrinsically funny – the only writer I can think of, except Lewis Carroll, who did so. There is a wonderful passage in *Martin Chuzzlewit*, Chapter 4: '"The name of those fabulous animals (pagan, I regret to say) who used to sing in the water, has quite escaped me." Mr George Chuzzlewit suggested "Swans." "No," said Mr Pecksniff. "Not swans. Very like swans, too. Thank you." The nephew . . . propounded "Oysters." "No," said Pecksniff . . . "nor oysters. But by no means unlike oysters; a very excellent idea; thank you, my dear sir, very much. Wait. Sirens! Dear me! sirens, of course."'

As Eleanor Clark points out in *The Oysters of Locmariaquer* (1965), which is not only the best book on oysters but one of the best books I have ever read on any subject, most of the references in literature to oysters have got it wrong. They always associate oysters, not with poverty, but with pearls. Oysters don't make pearls; at least, they don't make pearls worth having. Any old bivalve will build up a coating of something resembling a pearl around an intrusive object that annoys it; but it won't be pretty or valuable. The creature that produces the best pearls is called *Meleagrina margaritifera*, and the substance with which it coats the grit in its shell is aragonite. It doesn't even look much like an oyster. I believe it is edible, though, as I was once promised (though never got), in the former pearl-fishing town of Broome, Australia, a taste of 'pearl meat'.

The association of oysters with pearls, though false, has been rich for literature. Eleanor Clark cites Shelley ('He is a pearl within an oyster shell'); Shake-speare ('Rich honesty dwells like a miser, sir, in a poor house; as your pearl in your foul oyster' from *As You Like It*, where 'foul' does not mean that the oyster is off, only that it is outwardly unprepossessing), and again ('The firm Roman to great Egypt sends this treasure of an oyster' from *Antony and Cleopatra*); and Swinburne ('Then love was the pearl of his oyster'; the remainder of this couplet from 'Dolores' is 'And Venus rose red out of wine'). She even cites Browning because he mentioned oysters repeatedly and '*never* associated them with pearls': 'Than a too-long opened oyster', 'And laying down a rival oyster bed', 'Turn round: La Roche, to right, where oysters thrive'. 'It took real intellectual stature to think of them like that, considering the set of the centuries before; it is rather grand,' said Miss Clark.

She leaves out of account, though, Saki's pronouncement in *The Quest*: 'Oysters are more beautiful than any religion . . . There's nothing in Christianity or Buddhism that quite matches the sympathetic unselfishness of an oyster.'

Though I used personally to feel like the chap in W. S. Gilbert 'who had often eaten oysters, but had never had enough', I now find it difficult to get through as many as a dozen, unless they are particularly good English natives or French *plates* (meaning simply 'flats'). I am one of the lucky people who has never had a bad one; I know from many first-hand accounts that that is a painful experience. Prudence helps. If you open your own oysters and sniff each one immediately, you will never eat a bad one. An oyster that is 'off' has an unmistakable smell; one whiff will convince you to throw it away. Yet the warning smell disappears rapidly and sometimes the oyster-opener is working so fast that he forgets to smell each one as he opens them; otherwise no one would ever suffer from oyster-poisoning. If you have had the misfortune to ingest a bad oyster, you probably cannot bear the idea of ever eating another one. But if you are brave and want to try again, start with cooked oysters, as mentioned above.

In both Europe and America you can now encounter the rock oysters of the Pacific – usually from New South Wales, Australia. These were originally from New Zealand and are two different species. The warm-water oyster comes from the northern part of North Island and is *Ostrea crassostrea*, similar to the Portuguese and American rock oysters; the deep-water oyster needing colder waters, and therefore less long-lived and less easy to store, is *Ostrea sinuata*, and comes from South Island. The fact that these have been transplanted to Australia and flourished there reveals one of the most interesting aspects of the culture of oysters: they profit (or at least *we* do, because their flavour and texture are improved) by being moved about. A pity this was not known in Lewis Carroll's time, as he would have relished the paradox of the transportation of the unmoving oyster:

Four young Oysters hurried up,
All eager for the treat;
Their coats were brushed, their faces washed,
Their shoes were clean and neat –
And this was odd, because, you know,
They hadn't any feet.

Lewis Carroll was slightly wrong. The infant oyster, anyway, does have a foot. In the larval 'spat' stage the oyster possesses a tiny foot that allows it to attach itself to another object – which is usually the shell of another oyster. Though classified as a pelecypod, meaning that it has a hatchet-shaped foot like a clam or scallop rather than being a stomach-footed gastropod such as a snail or limpet or head-footed like the octopus, the oyster loses its foot early in its development, and is condemned thereafter never again to move by its own agency.

Out of the 300 or so species in the world, we confine our attentions in this hemisphere to only four species of oyster. Chief of these, at least gastronomically in my opinion, is *Ostrea edulis*, the flat native oyster of Britain, though its 'gratifyingly extensive' natural range says Alan Davidson in *North Atlantic Seafood* extends from the Norwegian Sea to the Mediterranean and Morocco. The large-scale culture of this oyster began in the Morbihan in the south of Brittany, and is the specific subject of Eleanor Clark's book. But diseases such as the recent plague of bonamia as well as changes in the market have made many oyster growers change over to other species. The best *edulis*, I think, are Colchesters and Whitstables, of which I have eaten some splendid specimens in recent years. These have become rare and expensive, and I do not think I have ever even tasted a Royal Whitstable (or just plain 'Royal'), marketed exclusively by the Whitstable Oyster Company.

In the recent past, most of the seed came from France and was relaid. But this has always been the practice; as we have seen oysters benefit from a change of water. Even the famous Belons of France were generally grown at Belon, rather than bred there. Colchester Pyefleets, too, were from the celebrated fattening grounds of Pyefleet creek in the Colne estuary, where these Essex oysters have been relished since Roman times, and the Borough of Colchester has a document from Richard I defining the area from which they may come. Other well-known British natives come from Cornwall, where 'Duchy oysters' are also known as 'Helford river' oysters, Devon 'Yealm' and Essex 'Roach', though I don't ever remember being offered any of these in the thirty years during which I have been an avid consumer of British oysters. John Noble and Andrew Long are experimenting with *edulis* at their Loch Fyne oyster farm in Argyll. They believe they have found a reliable and good source of spat, oyster larvae, and hope soon to have a marketable crop of Scottish natives.

In France the district of Marennes-Oléron is responsible for 60 per cent of the country's production of *edulis*. The oysters are called by the name of the place where they have been grown, and other famous flat oyster names, says Davidson, are Arcachon, the Bay of l'Aiguillon, the Ile de Ré, the Morbihan (of which the oyster capital is Auray), the Rade de Brest and the coast of the Channel from St-Brieuc to Cancale. Belgium boasts the oysters of Ostend, The Netherlands Zeeland, and Denmark Limfjord.

Two other species are eaten in Europe. The Portuguese oyster, *Cassostrea angulata* (Lamarck), was formerly the most important after the native. Its range was from Spain and Portugal to Morocco, and its extremely frilly shell is still familiar to most oyster eaters. This oyster is more robust and faster growing than *edulis*, and came close to replacing the natives both in France and England, though recent bouts of disease have led to its being replaced almost every-

where by the giant or Pacific oyster, *Crassostrea gigas* (Thunberg). This last can grow to a huge size – Davidson says the maximum is a 'dismaying 25 cm' (10 in). In fact, smaller ones are perfectly delicious, as most of the oyster's taste and texture derive from the waters in which it is fattened.

The tale is often told of the introduction of the Portuguese oyster into France as the cargo of a ship named the *Morlasien*. In the 1860s the ship had to take shelter, against storms, in the Gironde river. An unpleasant smell caused the master to think that his cargo had spoiled, so he ordered it dumped overboard, where those oysters that remained alive found the waters of the Gironde so agreeable that they bred there, and eventually overtook the native oyster in numbers. Until fairly recently almost all *huîtres creuses* were C. *angulata*, even the *fines de Claires* raised in former salt basins, and the particularly delicious green-tinged Marennes (which get their colour from their diet of a special creature, which defies exclusive classification as either animal or vegetable, but which contains chlorophyll). Now even these, and the *huîtres spéciales* (formerly *angulata* grown with special attention in small quantities in oyster parks along with *edulis*) are almost always the giant *gigas*.

The fourth species commonly grown and eaten in the northern hemisphere is the American or Eastern oyster, *Crassostrea virginica* (Gmelin). They flourish from New Brunswick to the Gulf of Mexico; and they differ so much in appearance that it is difficult to believe that the Blue Points, Robbins Islands, Gardiners Bays and so on from Long Island, the unpronounceable Chincoteaugue Bays from Chesapeake

Native French flat oysters – a bargain at 60 francs for 12!

Bay, and the Cape Cod Wellfleets, Warehams or Chathams are all the same species. I have eaten as many as thirteen different named varieties of American oyster at a single sitting at the Grand Central Station Oyster Bar in Manhattan. They all tasted much more like each other than any of them tasted like a European oyster, let alone an O. *edulis*. But their shells were fantastic in appearance, with all the colours of the ocean floor represented on one plate, and so different in size that one might have imagined that some of them were different creatures altogether. This begs the question: are *any* of them as good to eat as those from the other side of the Atlantic? The answer, I'm sorry to say, is no.

But any oyster is better than no oyster at all, even the Sydney rock oyster that is now opened at a central depot in New South Wales and there *washed*, so that every trace of briny flavour disappears down the Aussie plughole. Some say you can understand this once you've seen the pollution levels on Bondi Beach; others point out that central distribution keeps the price of oysters down so that they are still a working man's food in Australia. Oyster poisoning is, I believe, unknown. Still, I once managed to eat a Sydney rock oyster fresh from the sea (I opened it myself, which may be against the law for all I know). It was wonderful, pure essence of the Pacific.

One of the reasons the *gigas* oyster is available the year round (as was the Portuguese) is that, on the whole, it does not breed in British or northern French waters, so it is never out of season. I'm not altogether convinced that the breeding season is the only reason O. *edulis* is not eaten in months that lack the letter 'R' – they are, after all, the warmer months when it was dangerous to transport shellfish before there was refrigeration. But it is true that *edulis* is larviparous, and lays its eggs inside its valves, keeping them inside the parent for a week following fertilisation. The late Tom Stobart wrote in *The Cook's Encyclopaedia* that this made them 'nasty to eat in the breeding season'; it only makes the oyster unpleasantly milky, as the shells are scarcely formed when the babies are expelled from the parent.

The *Crassostrea* species are oviparous, and cast their eggs on the waters to be fertilised – as Eleanor Clark puts it. The fascinating part of the oyster's sex life is that it changes sex, and the self same oyster is sometimes a father and sometimes a mother. M. F. K. Fisher in *The Art of Eating* explains the sex change, in 'Consider the Oyster': 'For about a year this oyster – *our* oyster – is a male, fertilising a few hundred thousand eggs as best he can without ever knowing whether they swim by or not. Then one day, maternal longings surge between his two halves in his cold guts and gills and all his crinkly fringes. Necessity, that well-known mother, makes him one. He is a she.'

Nobody but the oyster seems to know when it is appropriate to produce milt and when to produce ova; but every oyster produces both in the course of a lifetime. This might be expected to make *ostréiculture* an even more interesting vocation. But in fact, the oyster's sex habits do not affect the oyster farmer at all: he never needs to worry about whether he's got too many mama or too many papa oysters. The bivalves themselves see to the balance of nature; all that's necessary is that they be adults.

Millions of baby larval oysters are produced as a result of these unconventional pairings. The spat are free-swimming at first, and can even steer a bit by virtue of a cilium, that gives way to a foot at the end of about a fortnight's activity. Normally they anchor themselves to something, such as a cluster of other oysters, and keep up the attachment for life. 'This is known as their free-swimming or pelagic period,' says Eleanor Clark; 'they are carried here and there by currents, but grow a little hairlike rudder that gives them some say in the matter, and also, at the end of this vulnerable but perhaps happy time, a tiny foot with which to attach themselves to something, which they must do when the time comes or die. Once "fixed", as the process is called, the oyster loses its foot and swimming apparatus and will never move again under its own power; an awesome requirement, but then all nature fixes in some fashion, even if only in being existentially "engagé", and by and large there seems to be about the same proportion of will to

'Now if you're ready, Oysters dear, We can begin to feed.'
Tenniel's walrus and carpenter from *Through the Looking Glass* by Lewis Carroll

LADY LOUSADA'S OYSTERS ROCKEFELLER

Patricia Lousada is a first-generation American, now settled in England. Her mother was Italian, and she learned some of her best recipes from George Balanchine when she was a ballet student. She wrote this recipe for me for an *Observer* series on alternative Christmas feasts. The stuffing can be made in advance and the oysters opened in the microwave.

Serves 4–6
24 oysters
75 g (3 oz, 5 Tbsp) unsalted butter
1½ shallots, finely minced
½ stalk of celery, very finely chopped
40 g (1½ oz, 3–4 Tbsp *after chopping*) watercress leaves, chopped
40 g (1½ oz, 3–4 Tbsp) well-drained cooked, chopped spinach
2 Tbsp mixed finely minced fresh herbs – parsley, tarragon and chives
4 heaped Tbsp fresh soft breadcrumbs
1 Tbsp Pernod or other pastis (optional)
freshly ground black pepper

Sweat the shallots and celery in a third of the butter until soft. Stir in the watercress and cook until wilted. Put in a food processor or liquidiser with the spinach, herbs, breadcrumbs, Pernod and remainder of the butter. Process and then taste and season with black pepper but no salt.

Place the oysters, hinge end down, in a 5-cm (2-in) deep dish. Cover with microwave wrap and cook (in microwave) on high for 4 minutes. (Give any oysters that haven't opened 1 more minute.) Allow them to cool enough to handle and remove the oysters and pry them open with a blunt knife. Pour off a little of their juices into the sauce mixture. Free the oysters from their shells and tidy up any bits of broken shell. Place the oysters in the deeper, cupped half shell on a pan of rock salt. Stir the sauce until blended, then place a teaspoonful over each oyster. Bake in a pre-heated 225° (425°F, gas mark 7) oven for 5 mins, or until just heated through. Don't overcook!

GRILLED OR MICROWAVED OYSTERS

You can actually open oysters over (or under) the grill or broiler or even on a hot electric ring, as well as in the microwave on full power (though you must be careful to keep your face well away from any oyster that hasn't opened fully – see method in last recipe). Of course you have to contrive to keep the cupped side of the oyster down, and steady, so the juices don't run out. The usual way to do this is by balancing them in a hollow of coarse salt.

Whether you open your oysters over heat, or more conventionally with a knife, they are cooked when they are just warmed through. Too much heat, and they shrivel up and become tough little nuggets. The object of cooking oysters (besides making it possible for people who can't eat them raw to enjoy them) is usually to impart some extra flavour.

This should be as subtle as possible; usually a knife-tip of butter or a spoonful of thick cream with a pinch of cayenne or a drop of Tabasco (much nicer with cooked oysters, I think, than grainy black pepper) is quite enough. But a tiny quantity of chopped raw or cooked spinach, or white of leek, or minced shallot could be forgiven, provided it is put on to the oyster at a stage where it, too, can cook for a few seconds. So, having opened your oysters somehow or other, either pop the butter or cream on the already hot oyster, or prop them up properly, add the flavourings and put them under the grill just until the edges of the oyster begin to look a little frazzled.

HANG TOWN FRY

I have eaten memorable oyster omelettes in Singapore, and I think I dimly perceive in them the original of this San Francisco dish given by Mrs Fisher. The only reason I include it, besides that it has some of the status of a classic, is that Christmas is the only time of year that I can imagine anyone having the surplus of oysters that would be necessary before you'd even consider making a dish like this. Mrs Fisher doesn't say how many this recipe serves, and I think from the context that she thought one heroic man or two normal ones might demolish this omelette for their breakfast with 'two or three links of tiny browned breakfast sausages and shoestring potatoes'. It will serve three or four New Men or Women.

On kitchen paper you dry 2 dozen medium oysters, season them with salt and pepper, roll in flour, then dip in beaten egg and dredge in fine white breadcrumbs. Fry to a golden brown on one side only in butter in a hot frying pan. Then you add to the pan 4–5 lightly beaten eggs, and leave to set for one minute, before turning the whole omelette to brown on the other side: 'The resulting dish will look like an egg pancake with oysters mixed in.' This is just the thing for New Year's Day breakfast.

CHAPTER THREE

The second course

Extravagance is a necessary part of feasting. The courses must be more numerous than for an ordinary meal, but also more lavish. This is true even in institutions. Raw army recruits are given a special meal at Christmas (one regiment where I witnessed the officers serving lunch to their men allowed two pints of lager to each squaddie, and the turkey wasn't even overcooked). In prison, where policy demands that treats are rare, Christmas is marked by a meal of better quality food. Indeed, on Christmas Day in the workhouse, as Sims's poem tells us (see pages 28 29), 'the guardians and their ladies . . . put pudding on pauper plates'. As for the paupers, 'so long as they fill their stomachs,/What matter it whence it comes?'.

Whether the festive meal is eaten on Christmas Eve, or is lunch or dinner, it characteristically has at least one extra course. In the USA, where there is usually only an 'entrée' (called this, presumably, because normally it is the start to the meal, though it is always the main course) and dessert, almost every family has an appetiser course. In France and Britain, as in most of Europe where three courses are often the pattern of the meal, at least one extra course is inserted between the starter and principal dish.

For many English-speaking families, this means merely that a solid dish is consumed before or after the soup. In the case of my squaddies, this was cream of tomato; a more fussy choice would probably not have been welcomed by these hundreds of hungry 17-year-old boys. At many private tables, however, this is the time for a seafood bisque, a consommé or a hearty game soup – even if they come out of tins.

At this point in the feast, though, the dependable French eat *boudin blanc*, white pudding. At least, they do nowadays. Some sources say they used to eat plain old *boudin*, blood or black pudding. In one of her wonderfully quirky notes to her translation of Brillat-Savarin's *The Physiology of Taste*, M. F. K. Fisher reminds us that 'in Paris spicy *boudin* used to be served on Christmas Eve. It seems to me that a little earlier in the year it was brought around, sizzling and rich and *free*, in the larger cafés of Burgundy. And I remember that the prostitutes would snatch at it, daintily of course but with avidity, as if it could give them some magic strength. If the waiter liked them they could have two or three pieces, and for once there would be no joking about the bulls it had been drawn from. Each fashionably thin pale woman would eat-eat-eat, in a silence straight from *The Golden Bough*.'

Lest there be any doubt that *boudin*, the black one, was, as Robert Courtine says (in *The Hundred*

Glories of French Cooking, which sounds so much better as the original *Cent Merveilles de la Cuisine Française*), 'for a long while one of the indispensable concomitants of Christmas feasts', he gives Achille Ozanne's verse-recipe for it. It begins: '*Préparez des oignons, hachés menus, menus.*'

Extraordinarily, I have two translations of these verses by this poet-cook in front of me; but I think I can improve (the sense), though prosaically, on both:

Prepare the onions, mince them fine,
Add them to their own weight in fat over a gentle
    flame,
Stir them, until they become golden,
And their sweet aroma invades the whole
    space . . .
Mix everything with the blood, then season well
With salt, pepper, nutmeg and any other spices;
A glass of Cognac; after this: you stuff it
Into the pig's intestine, one end of which you've
Tied in advance, and when you've filled it,
Tie up the other end, and into barely simmering
    water
Plunge all your *boudins*! These labours finished,
Drain them after twenty minutes' cooking.

Courtine's version goes on with a quatrain about lazing in front of the Yule log while the black puddings simmer. And the 1960 edition of *Larousse Gastronomique* says explicitly: 'Black pudding is the traditional French dish served at supper after Christmas midnight mass. Large quantities of both black and white puddings are eaten at this meal.'

In his *The Food of France* (1958) Waverley Root said, in his chapter on the Touraine: '*Boudin blanc* comes under the head of *charcuterie*, and you may find it listed with the hors d'oeuvre on a bill of fare, though it is more likely to be offered as one of the principal dishes. You will find this name on menus throughout the country, especially at the Christmas and New Year holiday season, when *boudin blanc* and *boudin noir* (blood pudding) are traditionally paired on *réveillon* menus (they are unfortunately disappearing under the influence of the commercialisation of these two midnight feasts, whose exaggerated prices restaurants have a habit of justifying by forsaking the hearty old dishes for what they consider more elegant and more expensive new ones).'

Larousse thinks that black pudding is of Assyrian origin, 'one of the few Assyrian dishes which have come down to us still greatly resembling those made by the pork butchers of Tyre, who, it is said, excelled in this type of preparation'. Though Courtine, who has written the 'Plaisirs du Table' column for *Le Monde* since 1949 using the nom de plume 'La Reynière', wrote the preface for that edition of *Larousse Gastronomique* (for which Patience Gray made some of the translations), he disagrees about the origins of black pudding. He queries its attribution to the Assyrians and Phoenicians, and even to the Greek cook Aphtonetes: 'Certainly there were preparations based on blood already in existence before Aphtonetes, such as the Spartans' black broth, the *myma* of Epaenetes, and the recipe given by the cook Erasistrates for a certain *hyposphagma*, which was a cooked mixture of blood, honey, cheese, salt, caraway and silphium.' (Silphium was a herb cherished by Roman cooks. An idea of its taste and smell can be given by the fact that, when it became scarce, the sulphurous, evil-smelling asafoetida was substituted for it.)

'Blood drinking, or eating,' says Reay Tannahill in *Food in History*, 'has been common in pastoral communities throughout most of recorded history. Before Islam laid a taboo on it, the Arabs were fond of a composite dish of camel hair and blood mixed together and then cooked on the fire.' I think we might draw the culinary equivalent of a veil across the rest of the history of blood-eating, until we come to the point: 'In Tyrone and Derry the blood was preserved for the lean months by being allowed to thicken in layers "strewn with salt until a little mound was formed, which was cut up into squares and laid by for use as food in the scarce time of year".' This is recognisably the ancestor of black pudding, and, says Mrs Tannahill in a note, drisheen, a kind of black pudding still eaten today in County Cork.

Courtine enquires into the etymology of *boudin*. He speculates on its relation to Old French *boudine* ('big belly, swelling') and to the Spanish word for the dish, *embutinos*. He asks: 'Which came first, "pudding" or *boudin*? The word "pudding" on its own does not imply the use of blood, you may say.' Here he is wrong. The *Oxford English Dictionary*, in a long, learned note, surveys the difficulties of connecting 'pudding' with *boudin* and concludes that, in spite of the different forms, they are very likely identical. And the very first entry for 'pudding' (a word that occupies several columns of the *OED*) gives it in the sense of black pudding. Both the French and the English words became current in the 13th century.

You can, says Courtine, with absolute correctness, make *boudin* with all sorts of stuffings: rabbit, cray-fish, meat, game, even bread; and some white *boudins* 'are no more than what the French think of as "pudding" stuffed into an intestine'. The great Ali-Bab, indeed, gives recipes for many of these in the definitive *Gastronomie Pratique* (1928).

The questions to be answered are why did (or do) the French eat black pudding at Christmas, and how did it come to be replaced (if it was) with *boudin blanc*? Courtine gets close to the answer. First he does a sort of round-up of recipes. The classic recipe uses one quart (1 litre) of blood to a pound (½ kg) of onions, a pound of fresh, finely chopped pork fat, a cup of cream (⅓ pint, 250 ml), a handful of breadcrumbs, salt, pepper, fennel and parsley. Variations abound – Larousse gives 15, both black and white, and the Gault et Millau *Guide Gourmand de la France* (the best book of its kind ever written) gives 18, but not all of them involve blood or even meat.

Waverley Root, I think, got his generalisations about the recipe for *boudin blanc* slightly wrong: 'Like *boudin noir*, *boudin blanc* is a soft sausage, and its stuffing in most parts of the country is composed largely of bread.' His specific remarks, however, are, as always, trustworthy: 'In the Touraine, the bread is replaced by breast of chicken. The Touraine *boudin blanc* is thus the finest variety of this sausage to be found, and there is a further refinement called *boudin de volaille à la Richelieu*.' Root is amused because Richelieu, despite its gastronomic fame for several sorts of *charcuterie*, had a population in the 1950s of less than 2,000. The recipe used in this tiny village is for *boudin* 'in which truffles and mushrooms are combined with the white chicken meat, and all of them are creamed together in an elaborate sauce. By

53

the time this has been done, one hardly dares refer to the product any longer as a sausage; it is more of a chicken croquette.'

Courtine lists Poitou, where spinach is added, Lyon where the cream and breadcrumbs are omitted but red pepper is used; and even a recipe involving a small glass of rum and a pinch of sugar. Then he gets on the real trail:

'The best *boudin* of all is in fact the simplest: that of the "*Tua*," as they call the annual pig-killing in those country districts where they also refer to the pig himself, with great respect, as "Monsieur." And the death of Monsieur is at once a ritual celebration and an act of grace toward the dispenser of all food.

'The literature of folklore is full of fine pages on this December death, the prelude to the celebration of the Nativity. In the crib, we read, He lay between the ox and the ass. But where was the pig, that encyclopaedic animal, that divine gift to man's appetite? Without a pig the crib is empty.'

This stunningly Franco-centric view of the universe overlooks that fact that where He was born pigs were not kept and eating them was forbidden. Jesus was, after all, subject to the Mosaic dietary laws.

One of the reasons for the formulation of the Jewish dietary laws might well have been connected with *boudin* and the reasons the modern French eat it at Christmas. There is a respectable theory that the dietary laws of *kashrut* were not promulgated (at any rate solely) for hygienic reasons, but to keep the Hebrews apart from their neighbours, by making them view some of the food of their neighbours as unclean. Thus the Jews acquired holiness by abstaining from these foods. Dionysus, the god of pagan revels, whom we

At the Market by Joachim Beuckelaer (c.1530–73)

know to have had Middle Eastern origins, is often pictured not only with his wine glass or flagon, but with a ring of sausages around his neck.

Sausages, of which *boudin* is the prototype, have been the food of revelry since antiquity. The medieval Christian Church took over the *boudin* with the rest of the midwinter festival; the killing time was assimi-

part of the Blenheim Estate, I have concluded that the apple is a Blenheim Orange. I've planted Cox's Orange Pippin, James Grieve, Egremont Russet (my favourite eating apple) and a few others to supplement the apples that were here when we arrived. But we are lucky to live at the beginning of an apple renaissance. In 1991 the British supermarket chains began selling formerly rare varieties of apple in season; and the same thing is happening in America, where the farmers' markets are introducing city dwellers to the extraordinary gastronomic rewards to be had from older types of our commonest fruit.

There is a temptation to say 'Hurrah, no more Red Delicious, no more Golden Delicious'. But I have one tree of each of these, and have discovered that they can be a treat when well grown and harvested only when ripe. The one apple I would banish from my garden is the Bramley's Seedling. Gross, bloated and sour, this common English cooker has no purpose I can see that is not better served by one of its fellows. With the very big exception of the various reinettes, French apples are boring, as are most American commercial varieties. Again, Jonathans, McIntoshes and Winesaps can be delicious, but everything depends on the conditions in which they are grown. This is why almost any variety grown in Washington state will have merit, and why even the wonderful Granny Smith tastes only of water and cotton wool when grown elsewhere in the USA.

Just think, though. We are one of the first generations since our great-grandparents to have the thrill, in the run-up to Christmas, of choosing the contents of the fruit bowl from a list of apples whose very names are poetry. Adam's Pearmain and Autumn Pearmain, Ashmead's Kernel and Beauty of Bath; Belle de Boskoop, Court Pendu Plat, Crispin and D'Archy Spice; Devonshire Quarrenden, Ellison's Orange and Gascoyne's Scarlet; George Cave, George Neal and John Standish; Herring's Pippin and Keswick Codlin; Kidd's Orange Red and Laxton's Early Crimson; Lady Henniker and Lady Sudeley, Lords Burghley, Derby, Grosvenor, Hindlip and Lamborne; Merton Beauty, Merton Charm and Merton Knave; Monarch and Mother; Owen Thomas, Tom Putt and William Crump; Stirling Castle and Tower of Glamis; Peasgood Nonsuch and Worcester Pearmain. True, some of them are no longer at their sappy best at Christmas but we also have access now to the edible poetry of the tropics: the heady perfumes of mangoes and papayas, longan, lichee and rambutan.

THERE HAVE BEEN CHRISTMASES, I CONFESS, WHEN we have been jaded and so tired of turkey that we've treated the feast as a fast. A fish course makes a welcome addition to the festival table, of course; but there have been years when a large plump salmon has taken the turkey's place at the centre of the revels. In fact, this is standard procedure in most of Europe. Those cultures whose main meal is on Christmas Eve almost all have a meat-less fasting supper, where fish is featured.

Even in the Orthodox Church, where Christmas begins at sunset on 6 January, the Christmas fast is observed. In Russia 12 meatless dishes used to be eaten in memory of the dead. Called the Apostles' supper, it followed the long Advent fast, and its resemblance to the Jewish Passover meal was striking in the requirement to invite a stranger if possible, and to lay an extra place and pour one more glass of wine than there were guests. The traditional 12 dishes included *borscht*, roast carp, the compote of dried fruit called *uzar* and a sweet rice or wheat porridge called *kutia*. This last was weighted with symbolism. The bowl in which it was eaten stood for the crib; the cereal the straw of the manger; in the centre a hollow was made with a spoon to 'receive the baby Jesus'; the fruit in the porridge represented His body, the honey that sweetened it His blood.

Carp is *the* Christmas fish in central and eastern Europe. Catholic Poland has the December 24 Christmas Eve *Wilja* or *Wigilja*. This used to be an Apostles' supper on the Russian pattern, and many of the dishes are similar. In Poland now children watch for the first star in the sky to signal the beginning of the meal, at which an even number of people must sit down at the table, lest one of the company present die during the year. As always 13 is a taboo number of guests (the prohibition against 13 at table predates Christianity), but an extra place is laid for the Blessed Virgin, as the Passover table has a place for Elijah the Prophet. The menu is similar, too, to the Russian one, with *barszcs* using *kwas* made earlier in December by fermenting beetroot, water and black rye bread, served with *uszka*, ear-shaped dumplings; a whole fish, usually carp, possibly pike, Jewish-style; *pierogi* filled with pickled cabbage and mushrooms; and *kutia*, a fruit, wheat and poppyseed porridge, or poppyseed paste with noodles, and *kompot* of dried fruit.

German-speakers, whether Lutherans or Bavarian or Austrian Catholics, have their Christmas Eve carp simmered and served with a sauce made from beer, raisins and almonds, and a bit of *Pfefferkuchen*,

honeyed spice cake. Carp turns up again on New Year's Eve. This time it is certainly a mirror carp from the fish farms, with large scales, and cooked *au bleu*. Each person saves one of these scales to put in his purse, to bring prosperity in the coming year, for with it his purse will never be empty. Even when cooked in this way, as in Jane Grigson's recipe in her *Fish Cookery*, the creamy horseradish sauce is sweet with sugar and almonds. As Mrs Grigson says, 'a strange thing about carp is the unanimity with which it is treated by cooks right across the world'. The Chinese, the Poles, the French and the medieval English all agreed on the character of the accompanying sauce, as do all the Jewish recipes. 'I do not imagine a traceable connection,' wrote Jane Grigson, 'because I suspect that the carp recipes used in Europe are living fossils of the sweet-sour style of medieval cookery.'

The other fish caught in fresh water that is eaten at Christmas Eve is the *capitone* of Rome and Milan, which can be up to 1.75 metres (5 feet) in length. In *Mediterranean Seafood* Alan Davidson says these are simply adult common eels *Anguilla anguilla*, that 'grow especially big and fat, rather like capons and perhaps because they do not mature sexually in the normal way'. He says the Christmas Eve method of preparation in southern Italy (and in the South of France where there is a 'similar dish') is to rub the pieces of fat eel with garlic, and thread them on to skewers, alternating with bay leaves. You marinate them for an hour in pepper and two parts of olive oil to one of vinegar, before spit-roasting them for half an hour. Jane Grigson says you can do this sort of *capitone arrosto* in a fairly hot 190°C (375°F, mark 5) oven on a grid or rack in a roasting tin.

CHUTNEY MARY'S SPICY LOBSTER BISQUE

This madly luxurious soup is given a thrilling new twist in this recipe created for their Christmas menu by Chutney Mary, London's Anglo-Indian restaurant. This tongue-tingling, palate-teasing version of a classic recipe is a good example of how Anglo-Indian cuisine was created in the first place and is a very economical use of lobster.

Serves 12

1 kg (2¼ lbs) live lobster (you can use 2 small ones)
2 sticks celery, finely chopped
1 medium carrot, finely chopped
1 leek, white part only, finely minced
50 g (2 oz, ½ cup) chopped mushrooms
4 cloves
2.5 cm (1 in) stick cinnamon
6 cardamom pods, crushed
½ tsp anise seed
4 bay leaves
5 litres (8 pints, 5 quarts) fish stock
200 g (7 oz, approx. 1 large) tomato, peeled, seeded and diced
100 g (3½ oz, ½ cup) rice
1 pinch saffron
3 Tbsp neutral-flavoured oil
1 large onion, sliced thinly
2 cm (¾ in) ginger, minced
5–6 cloves garlic, minced
1 Tbsp cayenne or red chilli powder
1 Tbsp ground cumin
1 Tbsp ground coriander seeds

To finish

100 g (3½ oz, just under 1 stick) butter
300 g (10 fl oz, 1¼ cups) single (light) cream
1 Tbsp almond flakes, toasted

Kill the lobster(s) by plunging them into boiling water or stab them in the back with a sharp heavy knife just where the head seems to meet the tail. Put it into a very large (more than 5-litre) saucepan and add the celery, carrot, leek, mushrooms, cloves, cinnamon, cardamom, anise, bay leaves and fish stock. Bring to the boil and simmer for about 8–10 minutes, or until the lobster is cooked. Retrieve the lobster and, when cool enough to handle, remove the meat and put the cracked shells back into the soup. (Bang them with a mallet if you haven't already smashed them up while taking out the meat.) Dice the lobster meat tidily and set aside for garnish.

Add the tomato, rice and saffron to the pot and continue to cook over a medium heat until the stock is reduced by about half – to about 2 litres (3½ pints). In a frying pan heat the oil and sauté the onions until light brown. Add the ginger and garlic and fry for a minute. Then add the chilli, cumin and coriander and fry for another half minute.

Scrape this mixture from the frying pan into the soup pot and simmer for 5–10 minutes. Remove the shells from the liquid and pass through a sieve, or process or liquidise in a blender. Just before serving, add the butter and cream and re-heat, but do not allow the soup to boil. Serve in individual bowls, each garnished with some diced lobster meat and a few toasted flaked almonds.

JENNY LO'S CLEAN-STEAMED FISH

Jenny Lo's family are Chinese Christians, living in Malaysia. Their family tradition is to have a Chinese meal. They sometimes start with fresh crabs steamed with ginger, spring onions, coriander, rice vinegar, garlic and chillies, and deep-fried chilli and garlic tiger prawns. Then soy chicken with dried and straw mushrooms; rice-wine chicken with coriander, spring onion and ginger; tofu and aubergines stuffed with pork, fish and shrimp; pig's trotters in vinegar with eggs simmered in ginger, rice vinegar and soy; a steamed fish, such as this one below; prawn and cucumber curry; white rice and chow mein for longevity, followed by Hangzhou fish-head soup with ham, parsley and pea shoots. Dessert is green mandarin oranges from China, local pomelo and crisp Japanese pears, with coconut and durian ice cream for the younger guests.

Serves 4 as main course, 8 as part of Chinese meal
1 whole fish, such as sea bass, grouper, carp or pomfret
salt
3–4 spring onions, shredded
60–100 g (2–3 oz) fatty smoked bacon or ham, shredded
6 dried Chinese black mushrooms, soaked, stems discarded and sliced
8 thin slices ginger
3 Tbsp peanut oil
1 Tbsp rice wine (or dry sherry)

For the sauce
1 tsp cornflour (cornstarch)
1 tsp salt
freshly ground black pepper
4 Tbsp chicken or fish stock or water

To finish
2 tsp sesame oil
fresh green coriander leaves

See that the fish is ready to cook. Scale and gut, if the fishmonger hasn't done this, and bone, if you wish (though it will taste sweeter if left on the bone). Dry the fish and rub salt all over and inside it. Place it on a plate that will fit inside the steamer, or on a trivet, or on a set of crossed chopsticks, in the wok.

Scatter the spring onions, bacon or ham, mushrooms and ginger over the fish, along with one tablespoon of the peanut oil and the rice wine, and steam on high heat for 15–25 mins, depending on the thickness of the fish. Drain off the juices and add them to the sauce ingredients in a saucepan and stir. Place the fish on a heated serving platter; heat the remaining 2 tablespoons of oil and pour over the fish and keep warm. Bring the sauce mixture to a boil and when thickened pour over the fish. Then spoon on the sesame oil and garnish with coriander leaves. Serve instantly, and let the guests pull the fish to bits as they eat it with their chopsticks.

CHAPTER FOUR

Talking turkey

The poor old turkey has had a bad press since it was first domesticated. When we say 'he's a turkey', we are not only being rude about the third party's intellect, but we expect the second party, to whom we are talking, to laugh, and part of the joke is at the expense of the turkey, poor beast.

Turkeys are stupid, and highly strung, too. A loud noise or a bang will stampede them into the corner of their pen or barn, and they are perfectly capable of huddling together so tightly that the ones on top of the heap suffocate those under them. We speak of 'cold turkey', meaning coming abruptly off drugs or some substance on which we are dependent. We don't yet use the epithet 'turkey' to cast aspersion on a male's potency or virility; but we could do, because turkeys now have to be bred by artificial insemination. The turkey cocks, properly called stags, have been bred to be big-busted rather than stud-like. As a result they are too ungainly to copulate in the normal way, and tend to fall off the females' backs. We bred them to be big and ignored their eating quality. We should have seen it coming. As long ago as the 1930s one of André Simon's contributors to his *Encyclopedia of Gastronomy* wrote: 'A large turkey cock with sharp spurs is best stuffed by a taxidermist; it is an old bird to be avoided by all cooks.'

Dorothy Hartley's near-contempt for turkey (in her classic *Food in England*) was, she claimed, widely shared. She quotes an old saw, 'Turkeys heresays hops and beer/All came to England in one year.' (This country saying may be partly true. The first citation for 'hearsay' in the *OED* is dated 1532, when it was spelled 'here say', close to the time of the first appearance of turkey; but the controversy over hopped beer, when London brewers petitioned the Lord Mayor to forbid the addition of hops or herbs of any kind to beer, occurred in 1464.) The late Miss Hartley (1893–1985) dismissed the bird in so few words that she required a footnote to explain herself: 'Being a north-country woman,' she says, 'I have no enthusiasm for turkey.' In the appended note, however, she glosses herself: 'Northern farmers have chicken for Easter, duck and green peas for Whitsun, and a fine meaty goose for Christmas. Most northern farmers say that turkey is only like a big fowl.' Then, almost grudgingly, 'The best turkeys come from Norfolk.'

It was inevitable that the turkey, whose advantage over the better-tasting goose lies solely in his size and the ratio of his meat to his bones, would come to taste like boiled packets of blotting paper, at least in his most commercial manifestation. Turkey breeding and turkey fattening are now two distinct occupations.

The commercial breeder sees it as his job to provide chicks that put on weight as rapidly and cheaply as possible, and whose finished carcass has the appearance and weight desired by the Christmas and (now, in world terms more important) Thanksgiving market. The turkey stockman simply wants the bird that puts on the most weight for the lowest expenditure on feed. The customer, apparently, doesn't care how his turkey is reared or what his turkey tastes like, so long as it's cheap.

Just as this was bound to happen, however, it was also on the cards that a reaction would set in; that breeders would look back to older, tastier varieties, and that farmers would begin to farm their birds 'free range' and give them feed that would make their flesh more, rather than less attractive. The result is that we're living in the golden age of the turkey, where for a few pennies more per pound than the factory-farmed article, you can buy a turkey worth the eating. In Britain, and to some extent in France, the consumer can now choose from among turkeys of different races, and in the USA you can even eat wild turkey once again.

English turkeys simply were not cheap until Bernard Matthews came along, though the lower cost of imported birds made them much more accessible in the late Victorian era. To be sure, their price fluctuated. By 1555, C. Anne Wilson tells us, there were sufficient turkeys being sold in London for the authorities to fix the price, as they did that of other poultry, and the tariff was fixed at a massive six shillings for turkey cocks and two shillings eight pence for chicks. By 1572, she says, the price of cocks had dropped to three shillings four pence, and the hens, which always fetched a lower price, only one shilling eight pence. In 1898, J. A. R. Pimlott found (in *The Englishman's Christmas*, 1978) that native turkeys varied in price from five to 25 shillings per bird, and were in competition with turkeys imported from Ireland, Austria, France, Italy and Canada. Those from Italy could be had for as little as two shilling three-pence, and Canadian turkeys sold for only six or seven pence a pound, probably undercutting the cheapest English bird.

In the USA the statistics for turkey-eating are easy. No polls are needed to show that the percentage of the population that eats turkey at Thanksgiving is nearly one hundred. In Britain, however, gallopavo-phagy (turkey-eating) is not even now universal. In 1955 a poll showed that 41 per cent of people in Greater London, for example, had chicken for Christmas and only 38 per cent ate turkey. Since 1974, though, the balance has been reversed, reports J. A. R. Pimlott. From 1974–7 turkey sales remained steady at about ten million (which works out at one turkey per 5.6 people), whereas sales of chicken actually *decreased* at Christmas from the normal weekly figure of five to six million.

A poll conducted in November 1991 showed that 77 out of 100 Britons had the intention of eating turkey for Christmas. There was, unusually, no north/south divide on this matter; you were equally likely to be eating turkey if you lived in the south of England or in the Midlands or the north. But there *was* a class distinction: 82 per cent of socioeconomic group AB said they would be eating turkey. So if you are in one of the top professions, and are upper-middle class or an aristocrat, chances are you ate turkey for

Christmas 1991. (The poll was conducted for the British Turkey Information Service who, not surprisingly, do not give us the more interesting information as to what the other 18 per cent had for Christmas dinner.) Another poll, by Mori for *The Times*, asked respondents on December 27 what they had done at Christmas. Seventy-nine per cent said they had watched television, 72 per cent had stayed at home (rather than going home to Mum, or out to friends or neighbours) and 70 per cent spent Christmas Day 'having roast turkey'. Sixty-six per cent admitted that they had drunk booze.

Three varieties of turkey are reared commercially in the USA. The Bronze, with its rich gold plumage barred with white on the wings and edging the tail feathers, is the largest. An adult stag usually weighs 36 lb (16 kg). The Mammoth Bronze was, Raymond Sokolov says, 'the first truly American hybrid', bred at Pont Judith, Rhode Island. The White Holland is known in Europe as the White Austrian. Its plumage is pure white as its name promises, and the average weight of a stag is 28 lb (13 kg). The Bourbon Red is a handsome bird with rich red-brown plumage highlighted by the white wing and tail feathers, and an average weight for stags of 30 lb (14 kg).

Smaller birds are preferred in Britain, where the supermarkets experience a good deal of demand for turkeys weighing more than 14 lb (6 kg) but less than 20 lb (9 kg). The British consumer seemed to dislike the black pin feathers that speckled the carcass of the gamey-flavoured Black Norfolk, and it declined in popularity in favour of Bronzes and especially the (I think inferior-tasting) Whites. However, Blacks and Bronzes and various hybrids, with plenty of breast meat but leaner lines and more developed flavour, are making a comeback, especially with mail-order sales and speciality butchers.

It used to take about nine months to fatten a turkey for the table (before commercial feeds were available, and all turkeys ranged freely, chicks were hatched in late February and early March). Now day-old chicks are bought in late July or early August, and good farmers feed them on cereals and allow them to range as freely as is possible, so that they peck at grit, and eat flavour-making insects and plants. Turkeys are especially fond of stinging nettles, a plant introduced to Britain as a foodstuff by the Romans. The feed is, to my mind, the most important thing about a turkey, because you can taste the quality of the feed in the large amount of subcutaneous fat laid down by turkeys; if the bird has eaten fishmeal late in its life, it will taste fishy.

In America there is a demand for turkey all year around, in the form of roasts, escalopes and even sausages. The British eat a much smaller amount of these value-added products. One of the reasons for the higher US sales is the promotion of turkey as a particularly healthy meat, which, being lean and low in cholesterol, it actually is.

THE TURKEY CAN BE HANDSOME. THERE ARE GOLD glints in the plumage of the modern Bronze and Black turkeys, and I was surprised, on a visit to John Munson's turkey farm near Colchester, to see that the wrinkled necks of the Whites are a fetching Post-Modernist blue. Nonetheless, it remains a singularly clumsy bird, lacking the grace of the swan or peacock or the relatively streamlined shape of most game birds; turkeys are even less gainly than are chicken and geese.

Why 'turkey'? Naming this fowl has been difficult for mankind. We now know that turkeys have no more to do with the Levant than Apaches, Comanches and Blackfeet do with the Subcontinent. They seem to have arrived in Europe first in 1523–4 (says Reay Tannahill in *Food in History*) or in 1530 (says the contributor, H. W. Brand, to André Simon's *Encyclopedia*). Both agree that they were taken to Spain by Levant or Turkey traders, since Seville was a regular port of call as they plied between Spain and the eastern Mediterranean. The bird came from Mexico, where its Nahuatl name was *uexolotl*. Clearly, no Englishman could be expected to try to pronounce that; so the thing carried was given the name of the carrier and became the 'turkie cock'.

Still more confusion set in because, at precisely the same time, the Portuguese were bringing back the guinea fowl from West Africa, and Ms Tannahill thinks that the Turkish merchants picked up that bird as well, and brought it back to an England that had eaten it in Roman times but since forgotten it. Remember that the turkey we are talking about is the skinny Mexican bird, not the plump article we put on our present-day table, and you can see how the muddle arose. 'The guinea-fowl,' says Ms Tannahill, 'was not unlike a miniaturised version of the turkey in looks and in its reluctance to fly.' That is why turkey still bears the generic Latin name for guinea fowl, *Meleagris*, while Linnaeus also gave it the species name, *gallopavo*, showing still more confusion. Its first half means 'chicken' and its second 'peacock'.

This has led some historians to think that the turkey was an almost mythical beast, and that any 16th-century reference in English to 'turkey' really meant 'guinea fowl'. Not so, says Ms Tannahill. Cranmer's sumptuary laws, which he promulgated in 1541, and which forbade ecclesiastics to eat more than one of the 'greater fowls' at a single meal, 'classed turkey-cocks with birds of the size of crane and swan, not – as he would have done with guinea-fowl – with capons and pheasants'. Moreover there is another contemporary reference to a Sir William Petre, who kept his table birds in a pen in his orchard in Essex; and the inventory included 'partridges, pheasants, guinea-hens, turkey hens and such like'. There was even a grant of arms made in 1550 in which one of the heraldic devices was quite clearly a turkey.

One of those who made this error was E. D. Boulenger, whose *A Naturalist at the Dinner Table* (1927) was used by André Simon. Boulenger quotes the *First Part of King Henry IV* (Act II, sc.1, v.19), ''Odsbody! the turkeys in my pannier are quite starved' and goes on to say: 'One forgives Shakespeare for introducing a name that would have been quite unknown in the days of Henry IV, but one must not forget that he was referring to birds which we know as Guinea-fowls, two or more of which could be cooped in a pannier.' And, 'even later, in the 1633 edition of Dr Hart's *Diet of the Diseased* (p. 78), when we read "Turkies of a middle age and reasonably fat, are a good, wholesome, nourishing food, and little inferior to the best capon", it is obvious that the reference was to *Guinea-fowls*'. In his attractive pedantry, in fact, Boulenger has forgotten that the turkey increased in size very greatly from its introduc-

The Christmas Hamper by Robert Braithwaite Martineau (1826–69)

tion in Shakespeare's time, and that the bird in question was not a full-size modern gobbler.

Reay Tannahill has great fun pointing out that of the Old World nations, the Egyptians alone called the bird a turkey ('*dikrumi*, the "fowl of Turkey"') and she remarks that they were, after all, in a geographical position to have known better. We Anglophones were

almost alone, too, in confusing it with a guinea fowl, with the most unfortunate exception of Linnaeus, who in his zeal to name *everything*, made the turkey's scientific name as opaque as its vulgar one.

But the bird was destined to cause linguistic misunderstanding. The French, Italians and Germans were never under the illusion that the bird had come from Turkey. They thought it came from India. So the French called it *coq d'Inde*. Eventually the creature lost its apostrophe and became *dinde* (the hen) and then *dindon* (the cock) and *dindonneau* (the poult). Italians baptised the bird *galle d'India*, Germans *indianische Henn*. Best of all, the Turks called the turkey *hindi*.

Aha, you might say: doesn't this actually show that the early 16th-century French, Italians, Germans and Turks actually knew the New World origins of the bird? After all, the Americas, as Ms Tannahill puts it, 'stubbornly remained "the new Indies" long after the error had been discovered'. Well, yes, except that the Germans, the Dutch and the Scandinavians actually got more specific about the fowl, and began to call it *calecutische Henn*, *Kalkoen* and *Kalkon*, all suggesting that it had come from 'Calicut, the place where da Gama first landed on the south-west coast of India. The Persians also had a contribution to make, calling the turkey the *filmurgh* or "elephant bird"' (by which they probably just meant that it was quite large).

In this nomenclatural comedy, the Indians themselves got much closer to the mark. In at least one of their languages they called it *peru*, which is, after all, only a few hundred miles wrong. It reached India, says Ms Tannahill, in the 1820s, where it was received as a novel and interesting food. It had probably come to India via the Philippines, which was then a Spanish possession governed from Mexico.

On the linguistic evidence, the Old World was quick to adopt the turkey for its table. The joke is, as Raymond Sokolov points out in his superbly scholarly and funny book *Why We Eat What We Eat* (1991),

that the turkey consumed in its millions by Americans every Thanksgiving is *not* the direct descendant of the native American wild fowl: 'The first domesticated North American turkeys were, in fact, imported from Europe.'

When the conquistadors reached Mexico there were only two domesticated species of livestock, the turkey and the dog. Turkey was thought nicer to eat. (I can tell you from my own experience that the Aztecs were right about this.) Some authorities claim it was generally cooked with a little chocolate, of which more, later. Meanwhile in the Jamestown settlement (1609), the first colonists, who were, by some accounts, bone-idle and dependent on the Indians for their food, don't seem to have been acquainted with turkey. But by 1620 in Massachusetts, the Pilgrim Fathers were already able to recognise turkey. Naturally they sowed confusion about its name; but it didn't matter because the native Indians obligingly called it *furkee* in their own language, though it isn't clear whether this refers to a wild or a domesticated bird, and we must assume that it differed from the domesticated Mexican bird brought to Europe by the Spaniards.

Now here's the good bit: it was English colonists who introduced the Mexican turkey to New England. Norfolk breeders had got to work, and scarcely a hundred years after the Columbian voyages, English settlers were taking to the New World a new, improved turkey. Both the Norfolk Black and the White Holland turkeys, Raymond Sokolov triumphantly tells his American readers, made their way to New England from old England where they had first been bred.

The English breeders were busy and enterprising. It is said, by Sokolov among others, that 'the English custom of the Christmas turkey was established in 1585'. It is certainly true that there are recipes for what C. Anne Wilson (in *Food and Drink in Britain*, 1973) calls 'the Christmas turkeys of late Tudor and Stuart days' (they were 'sticked full of cloves in the roasting'), and there is more than one Elizabethan recipe for turkey pie – but the same books give recipes for bustards, peacocks, cranes and swans. None of these was everyday fare. To quibble just a bit with this particular date, though, except for times when there was a glut of imported birds on the market, turkey mostly remained a rare and expensive delicacy in England until well after the Second World War; but it was true that it had become associated with Christmas on the tables of at least some of the landed gentry even during the reign of the first Elizabeth.

Indeed, in England it showed that it is possible to break down the general resistance of the English to novel foods, for soon after its introduction in the 16th century, when it graced the tables of the well-to-do, it, says Boulenger, 'displaced in a very short space of time the peacock, curlew, bittern, whimbrel and other fowls of the air and the sea, which figured on most bills of fare up to the beginning of the 17th century'. Mind you, it stayed on the tables exclusively of the well-to-do for several centuries. It was long a dish for great country houses, where there remained the need for a dramatic-looking bird that would feed large numbers of house guests. At first, there was little call for it in London except at the grandest tables where large numbers were regularly entertained. But by the 1650s the wife of Samuel Pepys was keeping her own turkeys in London, and in 1659 his diary notes that she dressed and served up leftover cold turkey for his dinner.

Turkeys were walked to London from Norfolk and Suffolk in droves of a thousand by the mid-17th century. The trip could take as much as three months, and so it often began in August at the end of the harvest. The roads were often muddy and hard-going, and the turkeys were sometimes shod, either in bags made of sacking, or with actual leather boots. Geese also had to be driven to market; but these sometimes ferocious animals will not tolerate shoes. (Hence the expression 'to shoe a goose' for a thankless task.) So their feet were dipped in tar, which was then sprinkled with grit. J. A. R. Pimlott, the pioneering social historian, relates a tale of two peers of the realm who, to settle a bet, staged a race between a flock of geese and a flock of turkeys from Norfolk to the Christmas market in London. Though the turkeys moved faster, the geese won by nearly 24 hours, as they ate while they walked and did not need to stop for the night. Despite this prodigious movement of birds, and that the middle classes of the time ate a protein-rich diet with what we should consider to be too much meat, turkey was still hardly an everyday item of food.

The supreme 18th-century use of the turkey at Christmas was in the famous Yorkshire Christmas pie, the last vestige of the medieval 'sotleties' ('subtle-ties'), of which the best-known example was the pie with four-and-twenty live blackbirds baked in it. In the recipe quoted by C. Anne Wilson in *Food and Drink in Britain* this begins with a boned turkey, into which is inserted a goose, stuffed with a fowl, in

85

which is a partridge, and in it a pigeon. These go into a 'standing crust', sewn up to look like a whole turkey, and the sides of the pie are filled with chunks of hare on one side, and moor game or wildfowl on the other. Four pounds of butter are added before the very thick lid is laid on and the pie baked. The recipe concludes: 'These pies are often sent to *London* in a box as presents; therefore the walls must be well built.' Yorkshire goose pie is the same, but with the goose outermost, which means that the turkey, the second bird, must have been a small one.

The bourgeoisie really began to get a bite of the turkey around the time of Charles Dickens, and it was not until the 1890s that imported turkeys were cheap enough to grace the Christmas table of the average office clerk. In this century turkey was still smart in the era of the bright young things, smarter than chicken, anyway; and roast chicken was itself a very special treat for ordinary people in Britain until the 1960s, as the 1955 survey cited above showed. John Munson, an East Anglian turkey farmer whose family has been involved in the business for generations, tells me that he is certain it was not until 'well after the Second World War that most ordinary working men could put a turkey on their family's table'.

FRANCE WAS RECEPTIVE TO THE NOVELTY OF THE turkey and accepted it immediately, in contrast to the initial Gallic suspicion of the potato and tomato, for example. After its introduction to Spain from Mexico in the early 16th century, it spread rapidly throughout Europe. The first mention of turkeys found in her researches by Barbara Ketcham Wheaton (in *Savouring the Past: The French Kitchen and Table from 1300 to 1789*, 1983) was in November 1528. (Thus Grimod de la Reynière was simply wrong when he said that 'the first turkey cock to visit these shores arrived in 1570 and was dished up at the nuptials of Charles IX'; this passage, which misled historians for over 150 years, is quoted in Giles MacDonogh in *A Palate in Revolution*, 1987.) These earliest turkeys were six pairs kept as *pets*, by a 10-year-old princess, Jeanne d'Albret. She gave half their eggs to a nearby convent, so you can see why the number of turkeys grew so rapidly. At a banquet in Paris in 1549 for Catherine de Medici 66 turkeys were eaten; and by 1565 there are records of turkeys being bought in Toulouse for another royal banquet.

Clearly, in France it was also initially a bird for the well-to-do. Barbara Wheaton thinks that the reason for the rapid spread of turkey through Europe was that it could replace peacock as a roast for banquets, though she has never found a recipe in which turkey, as was done with peacock, was sewn back into its own skin and feathers to be served. But she thinks that turkey was enough like peacock that the latter could serve as a model for how to use the newcomer, which hastened its assimilation. One can see her point that as a luxury meat, turkey was a necessity at any ambitious banquet; never having tasted peacock, however, I cannot comment on the similarity of the two. But Charles Estienne, writing in 1564, wasn't so sure: 'It is very true that his [the turkey's] flesh is fine and delicate, but without taste and of hard digestion . . . And this is the cause why men use to powder them, lard them much, and season them with spices. There is much more pleasure and goodness in the flesh of a peacock.' (The English translation of his

In The Market (detail) by Victor Gabriel Gilbert (1847–1933)

Maison Rustique, or the Countrie Farme, quoted by Barbara Wheaton.)

Most of his complaints, though, had to do with the turkey's behaviour: 'Whatsoever he was that brought us these birdes from the island of India lately discovered by the Spaniards and Portingales, whether we call them cockes or peacockes of India, hath more fitted and provided for the tooth than for any profit. For they may rightly be termed coffers to cast oates into, a devouring gulfe of meate, and wherein there is no other pleasure to be taken, but onely in their

crie and furiousness when they are come to be great ones: or continuall cheaping whiles they be little . . .' This was merely the earliest of the turkey's bad press notices. About 1600, Mrs Wheaton discovered, Olivier de Serres complained that it was 'very frail when young, always greedy, and so stupid and brutish that it has not got the sense to avoid the depredations of men and beasts . . . Even the mothers kill their own offspring by walking on them.' By the next century, Mrs Wheaton points out, the poor turkey's silliness was so universally recognised that *dindonné* came to mean 'duped', like English 'gulled'.

Turkey was popular to eat, though; so popular that she found a 1557 menu in which turkey figured in two of the four courses of a triumphal banquet. It appeared boiled, served with oysters and cardoons, for the first course, and roasted and served cold for the third. The first recipes stem from the middle of the next century, and because the shape of the turkey lends itself to it, they usually incorporate a stuffing, most often a meat-based one. La Varenne's recipe from 1654 involves boning the turkey, leaving only the intact skin, with legs, wings and backbone still in place. The meat is chopped with that of some pigeons, plus veal, pork fat and egg yolks, to make a farce that you flavour with ground cloves and capers. The bird is reconstructed with the farce, then spit-roasted until nearly cooked. The cooking is finished by poaching the bird in a good bouillon with mushrooms, following which you make a sauce with the liquid and a chopped bacon and flour roux, made piquant with lemon juice and vinegar. Then, if raspberries are in season, you add them to the dish. Unfortunately, remarks Mrs Wheaton, the raspberries ruin whatever wine you drink. This recipe, incidentally, comes from La Varenne's chapter on simpler dishes for occasions when the cook does not have a completely equipped kitchen.

Other turkey preparations she has come across include little ragoûts made with the trimmings and giblets, and pies, such as one made with a turkey stuffed with young pigeons, the palate of an ox, sheep's kidneys and sweetbreads, cockscombs, artichoke bottoms, mushrooms and truffles. A 1767 *Dictionnaire Portatif de Cuisine* lists forty different ways of cooking turkey, roast, boiled and fricassée, and embellished with everything from anchovies to cucumbers. But by the late 18th century, the gastronomic supremacy of the truffled turkey was widely acknowledged.

Turkey eating *seems* to have been more democratic earlier on in France than in Britain. In the early 19th century, Brillat-Savarin (the lawyer and theorist of gastronomy whose dates were 1755–1826) said, in *La Physiologie du Goût*, his 'Meditations on Transcendental Gastronomy' published at his own expense the year before his death, that he regarded turkey as the biggest and, 'if not the most delicate, at least the most flavourful of our domestic birds'. He went on to say (in M. F. K. Fisher's translation) that 'it also enjoys the unique advantage of attracting to it every class of society'. As examples of turkey's classlessness he cites 'the vine tenders and the plowmen of our countryside', and by means of a rhetorical question claims that on a long winter night when these rustics want to treat themselves they roast a turkey over the kitchen fire.

When the hardworking mechanic or artisan gets a few friends together for a rare evening of relaxation, 'what is the traditional main dish of the evening he offers? A turkey stuffed with sausages or with Lyons chestnuts.' Finally, 'in our most renowned gastronomical circles', in those exquisite salons where even the discussion of politics must yield pride of place to considerations of food and philosophical conversation on the sense of taste, the most highly appreciated, eagerly anticipated dish of honour is always a truffled turkey. And in an arch aside, thought by his translator to be a boastful tease, Brillat-Savarin implies that if we could but read the entries in his 'secret diary' we would learn of the extraordinary aphrodisiac properties of the 'restorative juices' of the truffled turkey.

It is difficult to work out whether Brillat-Savarin was claiming that turkey was eaten often by all classes, which would imply that it was cheap; or whether he was simply saying that it is the meat of choice for celebrations in every class, which might mean that it was still very expensive. He actually gives the cost of a truffled turkey – 20 francs (this would be in the early 1820s in Paris, when a substantial meat main course in a good restaurant cost one or two francs) – but I should imagine that then, as now, the truffle cost more than the turkey.

Against this interpretation, Brillat-Savarin writes as though the 'fairly large trade' in turkeys is an important part of the national wealth because it is a valuable, expensive commodity. He says that raising turkeys makes it more easy for farmers to pay their land rents, and that young country women can increase their dowries by raising turkeys because 'town dwellers who want to treat themselves to a feast from this outlandish meat must give up their gold in return'.

Brillat-Savarin's speculations on how the turkey got to the French table echo Grimod's, which appeared in the 15 years between 1803 and 1818. Both writers were wrong about the date of introduction of the turkey into France, placing it far later than it actually was, and both attributed its naturalisation to the Jesuits. The order, said Brillat-Savarin, raised them in great quantity on a farm near Bourges, and that is why, he claimed, *jesuit* was common slang for a turkey. 'Nobody who likes baby turkey (and who in the world does not?),' said Grimod on the same subject, 'could possible hate the Jesuits; for it is said that we owe it to these good fathers (themselves no turkeys) for having introduced the bird to France . . . Ah! What in heaven does it matter where it comes from, as long as it is tender?' Grimod obviously had a thing about infant turkeys, though, as in another passage he mysteriously remarks: 'It is said that eating the feet helps you to sleep; but you sleep well anyway in the company of baby turkeys.'

Grimod commented sharply, however, that 'the turkey has become so common of late that no one dares serve it at table unless it has arrived directly from the Périgord and has been stuffed with several pounds of truffles'. Grimod, a scion of the nobility, could not tolerate this sort of snobbery, and said: 'True gourmands rise above prejudice . . . A simple turkey from the Gâtinais or from Orléans, when the flesh is good and white, young, tender and delicate, is in their eyes preferable by far to the Périgourdine, which is often dry and tough despite its rich sauce. It is thus,' continues the world's first professional food critic, whose withered, claw-like hands made him physically repugnant to most women (though not to his long-standing mistress, Adelaide Feuchère, whom he married over his mother's objection in 1812), 'with a little common girl, who, when she is blonde and fresh, dressed in the simplest of clothes, will appear highly appetizing in the estimation of the connoisseur. She will always be a better bet than some rich old dowager, dripping with pride and brilliants.' (The translations are all from MacDonogh.)

Both Grimod and Brillat-Savarin appear to have been slightly obsessed by the subject of turkey, and each gave the bird a lot of space in their almost equally rambling reflections on gastronomy. Brillat-Savarin, though, does seem to have taken a genuine interest in how the birds were farmed, and hit upon a truth known to the modern turkey farmer. Rain is dangerous for turkeys, and they dislike it intensely, although not for the wonderfully imaginative reason he gives. His researches revealed that the survival rate for domesticated turkeys on French farms in the middle of the 18th century was only 50 per cent; whereas by the 1820s it was up to 75 per cent. 'Rainstorms,' he learnt, 'have always been the worst disaster for them: heavy raindrops, beaten against them by the wind, hurt their tender unprotected skulls and cause their death.'

Grimod, however, took turkey-lore to the furthest reaches. What could he have meant by this? '*Method of Knowing They are Young and Tender*: You should put your index finger into the anus of the animal and suck it immediately afterwards, at the same time breathing in heavily. This trick never fails.' (MacDonogh translation.)

Brillat-Savarin is a mine of information on the turkey, not least because he actually shot a wild turkey, in the course of his visit to Hartford, Connecticut in October 1794, but was uncharacteristically reticent on the matter of the recipe for wild turkey, which infuriated his translator. Mrs Fisher's gloss is, as so often, better than the text itself. She tells us that 'the only living human being I have known who could speak casually of hunting, cleaning, and then roasting a wild turkey, and all that in the state of Arkansas' told her that the wild turkey is normally stuffed with cornbread and butter. 'In general, this woman said to me, hoisting blue denim pants over her flat hip-bones and looking Chinese-like over her straight lower lids, in general wild turkey isn't thought highly of and people who cook them at all slice off the two breast-meat pieces and fry them in good hog fat. (*Filets de coq d'Inde sauvage*, I thought), and they sure taste damn near as good as steak, she said. But if they are roasted they take a lot of basting to keep from being dry, and yes they should be stuffed.'

Ranking high in the literature of turkey-eating, however, is Brillat-Savarin's tale of the gallopavo-phagic prowess of General Prosper Sibuet, first aide-de-camp to General Masséna, who died a hero's death on the battlefield in 1813. He was a countryman of Brillat-Savarin's, from near Belley, in the Ain. 'Prosper,' Brillat-Savarin relates, 'when he was 18 years old, and had that happy appetite which is Nature's way of saying that she is busy finishing off the creation of a fine sturdy man,' went as usual one night into the kitchen of the local inn belonging to Genin. It was the meeting place of the old men of Belley, who went there to eat chestnuts and drink *bourru*, which

The American Wild Turkey Cock by J.J. Audubon (1758–1851)

is what they, and the people of Chablis, too, call the newly fermented white wine. (I can tell you that *bourru* is a little cloudy, very fruity and delicious, and seriously laxative.)

There was a beautiful golden brown turkey which the landlord, Genin, had just removed from the spit, and its aroma was itself a temptation. The older men, no longer hungry, paid it no attention. Young Prosper's 'digestive powers', however, reacted violently to its smell, and he boasted that, though he had just arisen from the dinner table, he was capable of eating the entire turkey. His bluff was called, in the outlandish local dialect, by Bouvier du Bouchet, described as a 'fat farmer': '*Sez vosu mezé, z'u payo*' – If you eat it all, I'll pay for it; but if you don't eat it all, you'll pay for the turkey and *I'll* eat what you've left.

Brillat-Savarin describes the contest: Prosper, 'the young athlete took off a wing very nicely, and swallowed it in two mouthfuls, after which he cleared his teeth by munching the neck of the bird'. To make a pause he drank a glass of wine. 'Then he attacked the leg, ate it with the same poise, and dispatched a second glass of wine, to prepare a passageway for what was still to come. Soon the second wing followed the same path: it disappeared, and the contestant, more and more active, seized upon the last of the four members, when the unhappy farmer cried out mournfully' (and in dialect) that he could see that the future general had won the wager, and that, as he was obliged to pay for the turkey, couldn't Prosper please leave a bit of it for him to eat himself. In fact, he not only restrained his appetite and left the table a little hungry and the rest of the turkey for the fat farmer, but had the good grace to pay for both it and the wine.

Alexandre Dumas *père* died in 1870, and three years later his *Grand Dictionnaire de Cuisine* was published. It is full of mistakes, but none so glaring, perverse or funny as those in his entry for turkey, in which the bird's name is almost the only thing he gets

right. He leaned heavily on the accounts of Grimod and of Brillat-Savarin, whose turkey-obsession he shares. He disputes the earlier writers' turkey-lore, mostly; and he tells almost certainly spurious anecdotes about them – all in the course of this single entry. In the first place, he insists that turkeys were known to the Greeks, and that they called the birds *Méléagrides* after Meleager, King of Macedonia 'who brought them to Greece in the 3,559th year after the creation of the world'. (I am using Alan and Jane Davidson's excellent translation of 1978.) Dumas is perfectly aware that *Meleagris* is the scientific name for guinea fowl, but he says that those birds are misnamed, for Pliny (in book 37, chapter II) gives an unmistakable description under that name of turkeys. Moreover, in one of the lost plays of Sophocles, he insists, the playwright used the device of a chorus of turkeys to lament the death of King Meleager. Dumas accounts for the absence of any reference to turkeys in ancient Rome by blustering. Why is there no mention of them? Perhaps an epidemic wiped them all out. The Romans raised turkeys on small farms, he asserts, and it is just too bad that history doesn't tell us what happened to them; but we do know, says he, that turkeys became so rare that the Romans kept them in cages, as we do parrots.

Dumas's best turkey story is about Nicolas Boileau (1636–1711), the translator of Longinus and greatest literary critic of his age. Dumas prefaces the tale by saying (falsely) that turkeys react to the colour red as do bulls. Boileau, he says, was attacked by a turkey as a child; when the turkey saw the red of his jacket, he became so enraged that he 'so wounded the young Nicolas with his pecks that the latter, no longer capable of ever becoming an erotic poet, chose in consequence to be a satirical poet and to slander women'. This was also the cause, claims Dumas, of Boileau's 'secret aversion to the Jesuits'.

TURKEY RECIPES ARE SIMILAR THE WORLD OVER, as they are still uncommon birds except in Europe and the Americas. They do exist in the Middle East, says Claudia Roden in *A New Book of Middle Eastern Food* (1985), where they 'range very freely and are small and tough, more like game birds. So they are usually stewed rather than roasted.' Turkeys are not common food birds in China and Southeast Asia, though of course they can be bought in Hong Kong, Singapore and other cosmopolitan areas; and imaginative Oriental cooks such as Ken Hom have devised recipes for turkeys using oriental flavourings and techniques. Except in hotels and restaurants, ovens are rare, still, in this fuel-poor part of the world, and roasting is an uncommon cooking technique.

So it was, says Elisabeth Lambert Ortiz in her authoritative *The Book of Latin American Cooking* (1969), 'until recently when industrialization brought gas and electric stoves into the kitchens of Mexico to replace the charcoal stoves of the past'. In the home of the turkey, only breads and cakes were cooked in ovens except for roast turkey itself, usually with a hearty meat stuffing. 'I was a little taken aback,' she writes, 'the first time I encountered it; it seemed such a double richness, meat and bird.'

In fact, Mexico has been faithful to the turkey throughout its history, though Mexicans, like us, now eat a cultivated bird that is quite different from its scrawny, wild ancestor. Diana Kennedy, in the 1972 revised edition of *The Cuisines of Mexico*, remembered when she first went to Mexico, just before Christmas, seeing the traffic halted in Mexico City itself as a *campesino* drove his flock of turkeys through the great city, selling them door to door in the sidestreets. She also recalled hearing the sound of gobbling on the flat rooftops and even in the new high-rise apartment blocks, from then until Christmas Eve; for each household kept and fattened its own turkey on household scraps. Mrs Kennedy maintains that even before the arrival of the Spaniards, the wild turkey, *quajalote*, was already roasted (on a spit, of course), as well as casseroled with indigenous foods such as tomatoes, chillies and ground pumpkin seeds.

Turkey is still a food of importance in Yucatán (though not so much further north in the direction of Mexico City where *gallinas*, fat hens, are preferred), and Mrs Kennedy cites a single 'modest' regional Yucatán cookery book that gives 29 typical recipes for cooking turkey. She lists turkey *en escabeche oriental* (which she translates as an onion and chilli 'souse', in which a large quantity of onions, sliced, blanched and briefly marinated in vinegar, is added with chillies at the end of the cooking time to a turkey coated in a paste of garlic and spices, and poached in stock, before being coated again with the remainder of the spice paste and grilled); *en relleno blanco*, with a 'white' stuffing that is, in fact, not white at all, but the same beef and pork forcemeat used for *queso relleno*, the now-traditional Yucatán dish of a whole stuffed Dutch cheese; and *relleno negro*, the 'black' stuffing of minced meat with a paste of burnt dried chillies and spices.

But of course the most famous turkey dish of

Mexico combines the bird with the other native ingredient that is South America's most important contribution to the world's larder, chocolate. The French eat turkey and chocolate at Christmas, too, but not in the same dish, and it is always amusing to see the astonished look on the Frenchman's face when he learns that this is one of the earliest known recipes for turkey. I had the pleasure of being the first to tell Raymond Blanc, chef of Le Manoir aux Quat'Saisons, in my opinion Britain's best restaurant, about this most ancient of turkey recipes. He recovered his gastronomic composure immediately, by pointing out to me that using a little chocolate in a sauce for game is not unknown in Europe, 'and surely,' he replied with Cartesian rigour, 'turkey was originally a game bird.'

'No special festival,' says Diana Kennedy, 'is complete without *mole poblano de guajolote*. It is prepared with loving care, and even today, more often than not, it is the one dish that brings out the *metate*: chillies, spices, nuts, seeds, and tortillas are all ground on it.' (The *metate* is a sloping piece of volcanic rock supported on three thick legs, to which village women apply their *mano* or *metlapil*, or grinding stone, to pulverise corn, chillies, etc., very laboriously. Mrs Kennedy says that when she wanted to take it to New York with her, her Mexican removal men jokingly called it a *licuadora azteca*, or Aztec food processor.) For the village fiestas, each woman is allotted a task. Some kill and clean the turkeys, some toast and grind the chillies, some prepare the maize, which has to be soaked and cleaned to make the tamales, others grind the spices.

There are so many versions of this dish that not only does each village and municipality have its own way of preparing it, each cook has a variation of her own. 'A few more *mulatos* here, less *anchos*, or a touch of *chipotle*,' says Mrs Kennedy, detailing the different chillies, 'cooked with the turkey; some insist on onion, others won't tolerate it.' Cooks in Puebla itself, the place the dish is named for, toast the chillies, sometimes using only *mulatos*, over an open fire and grind them until they're dry.

Mole comes from a Nahuatl word *molli*, which itself means 'concoction', or a sauce made from any of the chillies, whether sweet, pungent or fiery hot. 'It *isn't* a chocolate sauce,' Diana Kennedy insists. 'One little piece of chocolate (and in Mexico we used to grind toasted cacao beans for the *mole*) goes into a large casserole full of rich dark-brown and russet chillies.' Though people often think they won't like this dish, Mrs Kennedy has always found that her guests are surprised by how harmonious the sauce is without any spice or seasoning dominating – and I've never met anyone who could guess that the mystery ingredient is chocolate.

The origins of the dish are not known though some writers speculate that the Aztecs themselves were the first to combine turkey and chocolate. It is certain that they made a drink from chocolate, and Elisabeth Lambert Ortiz, whose authority is great in these matters, says it was a royal dish of the Aztec court. Because it contained chocolate, she says, it was not only forbidden to women, but reserved for the higher priesthood, the military nobility and royalty; and she says that Cortés, the Spanish Conquistador, was served turkey with chocolate at the court of the emperor.

Most writers think the recipe for *mole poblano*

(the name for the sauce; it can be served with chicken, pork and other foods, but is most often associated with turkey) was invented in the 17th century by a nun, Sor Andrea de la Asunción, sister superior at the convent of Santa Rosa in the city of Puebla de los Angeles. Diana Kennedy says the most often told version of the tale is that, wishing to thank the Archbishop for having built a convent for her order, she constructed a dish that combined the ingredients of the New World, chilli, chocolate, tomatoes, pumpkin seeds, maize and turkey, with the spices of the Old World, such as cloves, cinnamon, aniseed and sesame.

Elisabeth Lambert Ortiz doesn't think the nuns invented the dish, because she is convinced it was known to the Aztecs. 'All the same,' she concedes, 'I do think we owe the sisters a debt. They recorded the recipe, which might otherwise have been lost, and they substituted familiar ingredients for some of the more exotic herbs and spices used in the emperor's day. I'd be prepared to swear that in the past allspice (a native spice) was used instead of cloves and cinnamon brought by Spain from the East, but since the flavour is much the same, why fuss?'

Diana Kennedy gives another story of the origins of this greatest of all Mexican sauces, one that still attributes its invention to the convent of Santa Rosa. This time it was the Viceroy, Don Juan de Palafox y Mendoza, who was visiting Puebla and dining at the convent. The banquet was being prepared by Fray Pascual. 'Turkeys were cooking in *cazuelas* on the fire,' writes Mrs Kennedy, 'as Fray Pascual, scolding his assistants for their untidiness, gathered up all the spices they had been using and put them together onto a tray a sudden gust of wind swept across the kitchen and spilled over into the *cazuelas*.' This would account for the enormous variety of spices in the recipe. In Diana Kennedy's version *anchos*, *mulatos* and *pasilla* chillies are used with the turkey and its giblets, carrot, onion, garlic, peppercorns, green tomatoes, cloves, cinnamon, coriander seeds, aniseed, chilli seeds, sesame seeds, raisins, almonds, pumpkin seeds, tortilla, French bread and Mexican chocolate. Mrs Ortiz's recipe adds peanuts to that list.

In a way, the history of the dish hardly matters. As Alfredo Ramos Espinosa says in *Semblanza Mexicana* (quoted by Mrs Kennedy): 'Whether it was prepared for archbishop or viceroy, by the nuns or by the angels, the very thought of it makes your mouth water.'

However, as Raymond Sokolov points out in a different context to that of a cookery manual, it is very instructive that people have bothered to construct a pedigree for *mole poblano*. 'Puebla in the 17th century,' he reminds us, 'was a hub of novelty, just the sort of place where a refined nun would mix chocolate, chillies and imported ingredients such as cinnamon and coriander for a sauce to go with the great Aztec bird.' Others have noted, as indeed I have done myself, that the sauce that results from combining all these ingredients is reminiscent of Asian flavours; and Sokolov thinks it is even possible that 'our taste buds are hinting at an historical truth. Probably not, but the legend of *mole poblano* as an invented sauce concocted by a non-Aztec with non-Spanish and local ingredients is itself worthy of note. Even if the account is only a fable, it is a fable that shows how eagerly Mexicans embrace the idea of a mestizo or hybrid origin for the national cuisine.'

Harrods Food Halls, Christmas 1922

The points of worldwide culinary contact manifested in this one recipe are awesome. If you subtract the New World ingredients, you of course no longer have a Mexican dish. But the seasonings that are left, and some of the cooking techniques, such as thickening the sauce with rounds of stale French bread, would have been as familiar to the 12th-century Moorish cook in Seville as they would have been to the cooks at the court of King Richard I. As for the cinnamon, cloves and peppercorns, don't let us forget that it was in pursuit of these as well as gold that Columbus set out in the first place. The fact that he (and his successors) instead found chocolate and the poor old turkey turned out to be a bonus.

TALKING TURKEY
Cooking and Stuffing

I have come to the unhappy conclusion that a frozen turkey is a very poor second best to a fresh one. However, the worst aspect of freezing turkey is the effect the process has on its fat, and the less long a bird has been frozen, the less likely that its fat will taste or smell stale. So if you are obliged to have a frozen one, do try to make sure that it was only recently frozen and has not had ice crystals in it for six months or a year. Fortunately, most of the frozen birds sold in supermarkets are the current crop, and have only been frozen because of the inconvenient log jam that would occur if every single Christmas turkey had to be dispatched, plucked, drawn, delivered, displayed and sold in a two- or three-day period. Four to eight ounces (125–250 g) uncooked weight per person is a rough guide to the size to buy. Americans eat much more turkey than the British or French, who seem as interested in the trimmings as the meat. And leftovers are only to be expected, or desired.

If your turkey was frozen, the single most important thing to remember is that it must be thawed thoroughly and completely before you cook it. This is an elementary safety precaution, as turkeys are hospitable to salmonella bacteria. Salmonella is a surface organism, so it is easily killed on the outside of the bird, but less easily in the bird's cavity. So if you're worried, don't stuff your turkey, but cook the stuffing separately. Be careful, too, of cross-contamination, and wash all knives and forks that have come into contact with raw poultry in very hot water; and don't forget the cutting board. There is, of course, absolutely no danger if you check the temperature with a meat thermometer. When the breast meat registers 77°C (170°F), the turkey is safely and succulently done, whether it was stuffed or not. If you want to err on the side of caution wait until the thigh meat has reached 85°C (185°F); but the breast meat will then be a little dry.

Another precaution is to stuff the turkey only at the last minute before cooking it. Beware any recipe that tells you to stuff the bird the night before 'to allow the flavours to develop'. And of course, be sure your oven is working: it's a good idea to use an oven thermometer to take *its* temperature every once in a while.

There are two basic methods to roast a turkey, the fast and the slow. My mother, who never learned to cook, discovered that she could roast a turkey without thinking about timing or temperature by putting any size of turkey in the oven set at its lowest temperature at least a day before it was to be eaten. She was right, after a fashion; though sometimes the beast collapsed under its own overcooked weight and lost its shape. Certainly there was always enough gravy, as the roasting pan was invariably full up with the meat's juices. Of course the meat, having lost all its juices, tasted like boiled string.

My mother was of the extremely slow school of turkey cooking. The slow school preheats the oven to 165°C (325°F, gas mark 3) and cooks the bird for 33 mins per kg (15 mins per lb) if the turkey weighs less than 7.25 kg (16 lb); 26 mins per kg (12 mins per lb) if it weighs more, not forgetting to take the weight of the stuffing into account. Slow cookers generally start the bird breast down, and turn it right side up after an hour if it's a small bird, or 1½ hours for a larger one.

The fast school preheats the oven to 200°C (400°F, gas mark 6) for birds up to 6 kg (13 lb) and cooks them for 26 mins per kg (12 mins per lb). Larger birds go in at 180°C (350°F, gas mark 4) for 33 mins per kg (15 mins per lb). Don't forget to weigh the stuffing, too.

I use a combination of both

methods. I calculate the cooking time at 30 minutes per kg, and start the bird at 190°C (375°F, gas mark 5), for 15 minutes for a bird up to 6 kg, 30 minutes for a larger one. I then subtract that time from the total cooking time, double the remainder, and cook the bird for the resulting time at 140–150°C (175–300°F, gas mark 1–2). I am unable to be any more precise about the lower temperature because I cook on the Aga, and I start the bird in the hot top oven and then move it to the cooler bottom oven for the remainder of the cooking time. Naturally the temperature, especially of the bottom oven, varies a bit when the top oven is in use; but many people have reported success using this fast-then-slow formula to cook a turkey (or any other bird or joint) in gas and electric ovens.

In any case, the bird needs at least 15 minutes resting time in a warm place so that the juices return to the muscle tissue and the bird can be carved properly. I often give it 30 minutes, especially if the turkey is a big one. You can turn the oven off and leave the bird in it with the door slightly open, but I put the roasting tin on top of the oven, which is itself quite hot, cover the bird with foil, put a cloth over the foil, and cover the whole lot with a mixing basin or the stockpot. If you've cooked the turkey properly, this is the single most important step to ensure that the meat is succulent.

Another trick for making the carving more elegant is to remove the wishbone before cooking. This will give you lovely, even slices from the breast.

As the disparity between cooking times for the white meat and dark meat shows, cooking a whole turkey is not the ideal way to go about it. But if your family insists on seeing it in its glorious integrity, you're stuck with one of the methods above. If, on the other hand, they will only see carved turkey on a platter, take my advice. Be ruthless. Amputate the legs and thighs, and cook them at the same time, but by the side of the breast and back, not attached to them. Or compromise by almost but not quite severing the legs and thighs. Put the bird in the widest cooking vessel you can find, so that the semi-detached legs can cook splayed out from the body. Best of all, cook only the breast and wings, and save the dark meat to grill and devil later. (You do this by making a paste of olive oil, crushed garlic, Dijon mustard and cayenne, which you rub into the superficially slashed thighs and drumsticks before you grill them.)

If you're bold enough to do this, you might consider cooking the dark meat and light meat in two different preparations (see the recipes on page 100). Or you could bone the turkey completely, place it skin-side down on the cutting board, season it, roll it up into a sausage shape with the stuffing, and sew up the back. You can either leave it as a sausage or make it into a vaguely bird-shaped parcel.

THE STUFFING

Almost anything except chocolate bars or ice cream can be used to stuff a turkey, but it's not a very good idea. Tradition dictates that the stuffing should be based on something starchy, generally stale bread (but rice, wild rice, chestnuts or cooked potatoes are all possible), bound with egg, and incorporating something fatty (oil or butter), something meaty (the liver, sautéed just until stiff, then cubed; or ham, bacon, sausagemeat, wild or cultivated mushrooms, or oysters, which are best of all), something aromatic (onions, garlic), something crunchy (celery, walnuts, hazelnuts or pistachios) and some herbs (I like thyme best of all, and lovage or sage is very nice in small quantities).

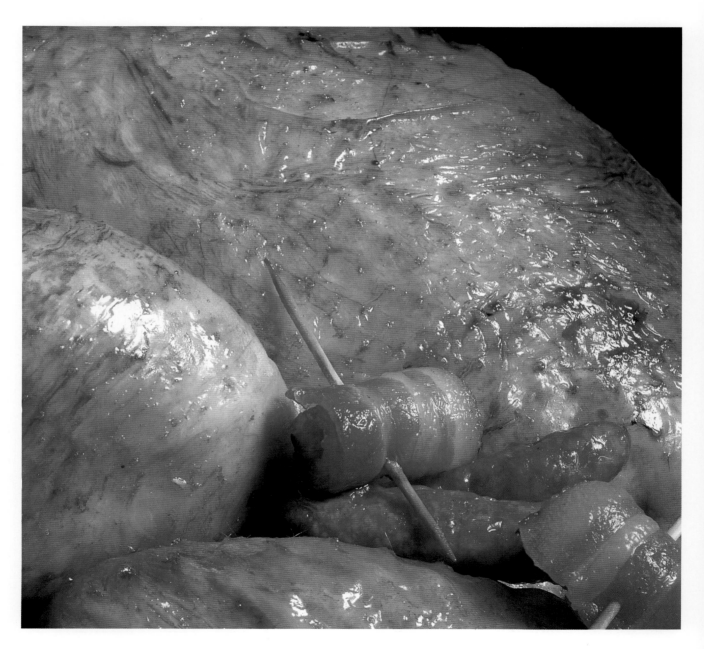

Fannie Farmer, author of the first standard American cookbook, says you will need about ¾ cup per lb or 9 cups of stuffing for a 12 lb turkey. These quantities are obviously untranslatable into metric or Imperial measures and, in any case, make very little sense unless you know the density of the stuffing. The most practical advice is to make up whatever quantity of stuffing you feel like making. If it is too little, that's fine, as it is imperative that the bird be stuffed loosely. If it's too much, cook the surplus separately in a buttered or oiled dish. You can stuff both the gut cavity and the neck cavity; and, of course, you can use two different stuffings, providing they are complementary in flavour.

Game birds such as pheasant often have a few packets of a soft white cheese such as *petit suisse* placed in the cavity with some salt and pepper. They melt and lubricate the bird very deliciously. Obviously you can do this with turkey, but you'll need a hell of a lot of cheese. It might be more sensible to do as the French sometimes do, and place a few *boudins*, previously blanched or stiffened briefly in butter, in the cavity. Both black pudding and white pudding are good; but I wouldn't use both, as the black ones will discolour the white ones.

I very often don't stuff the bird, but season the cavity and shove in a stick of celery, some garlic and onions and a sprig of thyme or rosemary, along with a lemon, orange or apple cut in half. The cooking time is thus reduced, and I think the result is somehow juicier.

THE GRAVY AND THE BREAD SAUCE

Roast the bird on a rack in a tin, or try this trick: slice some Spanish onions thickly, make a platform to rest the bird on and wedge it securely. You can vary this by putting coarsely chopped carrots, celery, shallots and garlic, sprigs of herbs, or even a properly constructed *mirepoix* of diced onion, garlic, carrot, celery and blanched bacon under the bird. Any of these will result in very superior pan juices, which can be served as is in a warmed *gras-maigre*, one of those sauceboats with two spouts.

Or you can make gravy (I never bother) by deglazing the roasting pan with wine, spirits, stock or water, and topping up the volume with more liquid. If you want thick gravy, add *beurre manié*, made by mixing together equal quantities of plain flour and softened butter. Add this a pinch at a time, and stir until your gravy is as you like it; then simmer for another 3–5 minutes so that the unpleasant raw taste of the flour disappears. Be sure you taste for seasoning before you put it into a warmed jug or sauceboat.

British cooks traditionally serve a dish of fried breadcrumbs and one of bread sauce with roast birds of every sort, including game. Bread sauce involves infusing milk with the flavours of a clove-stuck onion in a *bain-marie* for as long as possible. You then whisk in fresh breadcrumbs, usually white, in the proportion 90–125 g (3–4 oz, ¾–1 cup) to 500 ml (15 fl oz, 2 cups) milk, over the simmering water of the *bain-marie*. Jane Grigson advises adding more breadcrumbs if it is not thick enough (she says it 'should not spread very much when put onto a plate') or adding a little milk if it is so thick that the spoon will stand up in it. The traditional seasoning is mace and nutmeg, along with salt, white pepper and cayenne pepper. You finish the sauce by stirring in 2 Tbsp of butter or thick cream, and a sprinkling of cayenne over the top to mitigate its pale complexion. It's actually very good so long as you let the onion infuse long enough.

FRANCES BISSELL'S TURKEY IN TWO WAYS

Remove the breasts and thighs from the carcass, or get the butcher to do it, and bone and skin them. Cut the thigh meat (better than drumsticks, which are too sinewy) into regular-sized chunks and marinate overnight in a heavy plastic bag with olive oil, lemon juice and the rind of the lemon, crushed garlic, thyme, bay leaves, salt and freshly ground black pepper and some white wine. You can marinate the skinned and boned whole breasts in the same mixture, or slice the breast into thin steaks and flatten them further into the very thin *paillards*, and only marinate these for an hour or so, in the same marinade or merely in olive oil, lemon juice, salt and pepper.

Remove the thigh meat from the marinate, dry it, and brown it gently in olive oil, along with some aromatics, such as sliced onion or leek and celery. Then either stew briefly in the strained marinade, or in white wine. Add a bit of orange peel, if you like – and I should use a crushed dried and seeded chilli. As soon as the dark meat is done remove it from the heat and keep warm. If there is too much liquid, pour it off and reduce it separately so that the meat does not overcook. Add black olives, such as those of Nyons if you like them, in time just to warm through, and sprinkle with chopped parsley.

At the same time, serve everyone a grilled *paillard*, or thicker steak if you like, of the white meat. It looks wonderful if you heat a metal skewer to red-hot and make the *quadrillage*, the hatched grill marks on both sides of the meat.

KEN HOM'S ROAST TURKEY STEAKS

Cook the turkey in the usual way, anointing the breasts if you like, or putting butter between the skin and the meat (see Claudia Roden's Flavoured Butter, below). Allow the bird to rest in a warm place for 20 mins, or even half an hour if it is a big one. Then, working quickly, remove each breast (this is much easier if you have taken out the wishbone before cooking the turkey). Put it, skin attached, meat-side down on the cutting board, and slice off steaks about 2.5 cm (1 in) thick. As the idea is to save the carver's energy you will probably wish to joint, rather than slice, the dark meat, and then slice chunks off legs and thighs. Serve with *jus* or gravy made in the usual way. If you've cooked the turkey so that the white meat is still moist, this will give succulent steaks that are nicer to eat than thin slices.

TURKEY MOLE POBLANO DE GUAJOLOTE

There is a major difference in the recipes given for this dish by Elisabeth Lambert Ortiz and Diana Kennedy, in that the former first simmers until tender her 4-kg (8-lb) turkey cut up into serving pieces with onion and garlic, and then sautés it in 100 g (3 oz, ½ cup) of lard. Mrs Kennedy braises hers in the oven, without liquid, in 6–8 Tbsp of lard. Put the turkey aside and either save Mrs Ortiz's stock or, if you have followed Mrs Kennedy, make some with the turkey trimmings and giblets (except for the liver).

Serves 10

5–6 *ancho* chillies, stemmed, seeded and torn in pieces

6–8 *mulato* chillies, stemmed, seeded and torn in pieces

4–6 *pasilla* chillies, stemmed, seeded and torn in pieces

2 medium onions, chopped

3 cloves garlic, chopped

2 tortillas, broken up

3 medium tomatoes, peeled and seeded

20 almonds, unskinned

50 g (2 oz, ¼ cup) peanuts

75 g (2½ oz, ½ cup) raisins, fried in a touch of lard just until they swell

4 Tbsp sesame seeds

1 tsp coriander seed

½ tsp anise seed

2 cloves

1-cm (½-in) stick cinnamon

4 Tbsp lard

500 ml (16 fl oz, 2 cups) reserved turkey broth

45g (1½ oz) tablet drinking chocolate (if you can't put your hands on that, substitute the same weight of plain chocolate, or better still, American Baker's unsweetened chocolate plus 1 Tbsp sugar)

2 Tbsp pumpkin seeds, hulled, unsalted

You make the sauce by steeping in boiling water to cover, the stemmed, seeded and torn chillies from 30 minutes to a maximum of 2 hours. Then process them and their soaking water with the onions, garlic, tortillas and the flesh and juice only of the tomatoes. Reserve this paste. Start again with a clean, dry food processor, and put into it the almonds, peanuts, raisins, plus 2 Tbsp of sesame seeds, the coriander seed, anise seed, cloves and a stick of cinnamon, all toasted lightly in the same frying pan. Whizz this up and combine it with the chilli paste you made earlier. Sauté this in the lard, using that left over in the turkey sauté pan, if there is any, for 5 minutes.

Now stir in the reserved turkey broth plus the secret ingredient, the tablet of chocolate, broken up. Cook over a low heat, stirring constantly, until the sauce is the consistency of double (heavy) cream. Add more stock if necessary, and don't forget to taste for salt. Simmer the turkey in this, covered, for 20–30 minutes.

In a small frying pan toast the remaining sesame seeds and the pumpkin seeds and sprinkle these over the turkey and its sauce arranged on a warmed serving dish. Accompany with tortillas, rice, fried beans and guacamole.

CLAUDIA RODEN'S FLAVOURED BUTTER FOR TURKEY

Make this up in quantities to the size of your turkey. This will do for a bird of 5 kg (10 lbs) or under; double the recipe for a larger bird, and treble it for a very large turkey. Separate the skin from the flesh using your fingers, as gently as possible so as not to tear the skin. (Sew it up if you do tear it.) Start by loosening the skin of the breast, and you will find that you can easily detach the thin membranes that join the flesh to the skin of the thighs. The skin is more difficult to detach from the membrane at the back-bone and the ends of the legs. Simply massage the flavoured butter into the flesh, giving a thicker coating of butter to the breast, and roast the bird as you usually do. This is a slightly Middle Eastern butter, with sweet spices, and goes well with Claudia's dried fruit Turkey Stuffing (right). Almost any flavouring can be used, from garlic, parsley and grated lemon zest, to anchovy paste or finely minced black truffle, to flavour the butter.

115 g (4 oz, 1 stick) unsalted butter, softened
1 tsp ground cinnamon
1 tsp ground allspice
salt and freshly ground black pepper

Blend the ingredients well together with a fork.

CLAUDIA RODEN'S TURKEY STUFFING

This is taken from a recipe for Persian chicken stuffed with dried fruits. The quantity given will stuff a 5 kg (10 lb) turkey fore and aft, as you do not want to cram the bird to bursting. Double or treble the recipe as needed. It is also very good with goose.

2 onions, finely chopped
4 Tbsp unsalted butter
500 g (1 lb) prunes, soaked, stoned and chopped
500 g (1 lb) dried apricots, soaked and chopped
120 g (4 oz, ⅔ cup) seedless raisins
120 g (4 oz, 1 cup) broken walnuts
4 apples, peeled, cored and chopped
salt and freshly ground black pepper
2 tsps ground cinnamon

Sauté the onion in the butter until soft and golden. Add the chopped fruits, raisins and nuts and cook gently until they plump up. Season with salt, pepper and cinnamon, being certain to taste.

CHUTNEY MARY'S TURKEY NARANGI

This is an adaptation of a genuine recipe for lamb, which originated in the banqueting kitchens of the late Nizam of Hyderabad. This version was developed by the chef of Chutney Mary in London. This was, in fact, the way most Anglo-Indian dishes originated, with Indian cooks giving an interesting and always spicy twist to English recipes. Wild rice is the ideal accompaniment to this dish; and I found that, despite the strong orange flavours in the sauce, it was very good with a young, robust Italian red wine.

1 whole small (3.5–4 kg, 8–9 lb) turkey
1 bouquet garni

For the stuffing
1 large onion, finely minced
4–6 Tbsp oil
1 tsp each ground cinnamon, cardamom, cloves
200 ml (8 fl oz, 1 cup) single (light) cream
3–4 fresh green chillies, seeded unless you want some fire in your stuffing
150 g (5 oz, ½ cup) Indian *paneer*, for which you can substitute a packet of fine curd cottage cheese or dry curd cheese
150 g (5 oz, 1¼ cups) dried currants

For the marinade
4 heaped tsp chilli powder
salt
1 heaped tsp turmeric
100 g (4 oz, ¼ cup) fresh ginger purée, made in food processor *or* pounded in mortar and pestle

For the sauce
1 heaped tsp cumin seeds
2 heaped tsp ground coriander
450 g (16 fl oz, 2 cups) yoghurt
1 litre (1¾ pints, 1 quart) fresh orange juice, preferably from bitter Seville oranges, or made sour by 1 tsp lemon juice
2 Tbsp Orange Curaçao
6 oranges, peeled and cut into in tidy segments, with the grated zest of two of them

Joint the turkey into 4 pieces. Take off the wing tips, but keep the wing bone attached to the breast. Bone the legs and thighs and mince the dark meat. Put the bones into a stockpot with 5 litres (8 pints, 5 quarts) water and the bouquet garni. Bring to the boil and reduce to 1 litre (1¾ pints, 1 quart). Cool, strain and set aside.

Take each breast and wing joint and, holding the cut side towards you, make a slit in it lengthways so as to make a pocket to hold the stuffing. For the stuffing, sauté the onion until brown in 1–2 Tbsp of the oil. Mix this with the minced turkey and ground cinnamon, cardamom and cloves in the food processor with the steel blade fitted. Process to a paste with the cream, the green chillies and the *paneer* or cottage cheese. Add the currants and process briefly.

Spoon the filling into the slit in the turkey breasts and tie with string at regular intervals. Now smear the turkey breasts with a marinade made from 1–2 Tbsp of the oil, mixed with 1 tsp of the chilli powder, a big pinch of salt, ½ tsp turmeric and half the ginger purée. Allow to stand for 4 hours to absorb the marinade.

Roast in a preheated moderately hot (200°C, 400°F, gas mark 6) oven until the skin is light brown, about 45–50 mins. Then rest in a warm place while you make the sauce.

Heat the remaining 2 Tbsp of oil in a saucepan on medium heat and add the cumin seeds. Stir for 30 secs, and add the remaining 3 tsp of chilli powder; the remaining ½ tsp of turmeric and the ground coriander. After 10 secs add the rest of the ginger purée. Stir for another 30 secs and add the yoghurt; stir vigorously for another min. Now add the orange juice and enough turkey stock to make a smooth, flowing, thinnish gravy. Flavour it with the Curaçao, add the orange zest and simmer for 1 min longer. Off the fire add the orange segments to the sauce. Slice the turkey across the breast and serve with a generous amount of the sauce.

TRUFFLED TURKEY (EN DEMI-DEUIL)

Following the method on page 102 for inserting butter under the skin of the turkey, do so, with the addition of some brandy and finely chopped truffle to the butter. Then insert thin slices of black truffle under the skin as well, making as regular a pattern as your pocket will allow. Roast in the usual way, being sure to keep the breast covered with butter-soaked muslin. Rest before carving – at the table to show off your extravagance. And don't lose any of the precious truffle-flavoured juices, which should simply be served in a warmed sauceboat.

KENTUCKY HOT BROWN SANDWICH

This is the way we used up leftover turkey in Kentucky. The recipe was supposed to have been invented at Brown's hotel in Louisville, and perhaps it was. Good bread is toasted lightly, put into an ovenproof dish, topped with regular slices of turkey, usually breast meat only, and slices either of Kentucky ham or of crisp bacon. Over this open sandwich goes a cheese-flavoured white sauce, made by stirring either mature grated cheddar or a good grated Swiss cheese into a *béchamel*. A sprinkle of cayenne and a grating of nutmeg are both good ideas, and I'd be tempted to butter the toast lightly and smear it with Dijon mustard before placing the meat upon it. It goes under the grill till brown.

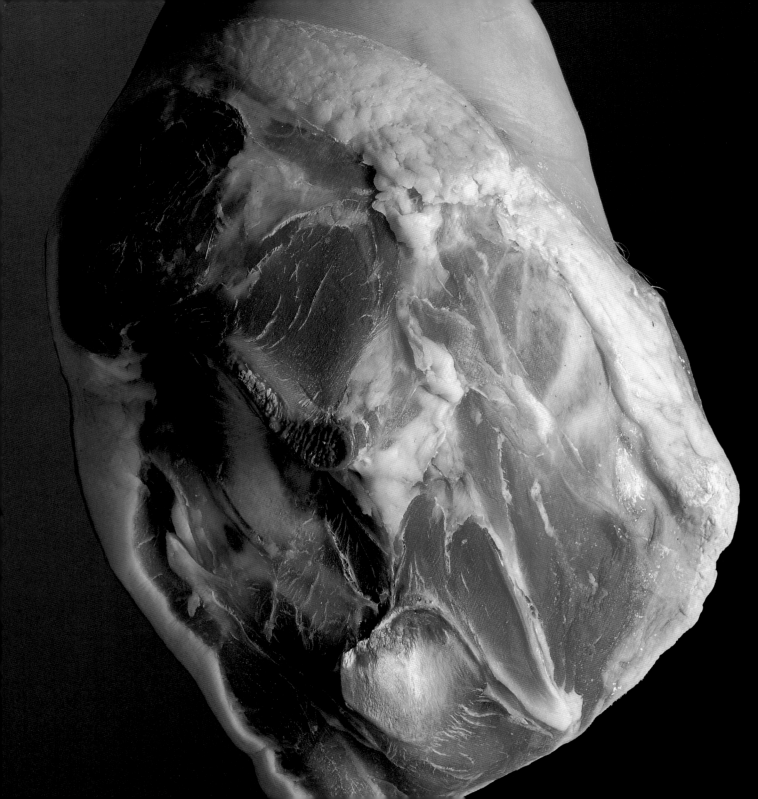

CHAPTER FIVE

Tired of turkey?

The Chinese say a duck is too much for one and not enough for two people to eat. Ultimately, this is the reason most of us now eat turkey at Christmas, for similar problems arise with the capon and the goose. None of the fat, succulent birds yields quite enough meat to cope with an extended family bent on gorging themselves.

Geese are not at their best at Christmas. 'A Michaelmas goose,' wrote Dr William Kitchiner in *The Cook's Oracle* (1820) 'is as famous in the mouths of the million as the minced-pie at Christmas; yet for those who eat with delicacy, it is, at that time, too full-grown. The true period when the goose is in the highest perfection is when it has just acquired its full growth, and not begun to harden; if the March goose is insipid, the Michaelmas goose is rank. The fine time is between both; from the second week in June to the first in September.' Whatever the time of year, the goose's own diet is of paramount importance to its eating quality. The first duty of a goose is to be plump.

The goose, in any case, was a make-do. The proper Christmas tradition was to eat a boar's head. Though it looked absolutely splendid, and could be accompanied to table with great ceremony and more than one version of a well-known song, the boar's head had its drawbacks, too. Your minstrels or varlets could sing:

> Hey! Hey! Hey! Hey!
> Hey! Hey! Hey! Hey!
> The boar's head in hand I bring,
> With garlands gay in carrying,
> I pray you all with me to sing
> Hey! etc.
> Lords and knights and squires,
> Parsons, priests and vicars,
> The boar's head is the first mess!
> Hey! etc.
> The boar's head is armed gay!

meaning it was properly decorated. Or they could sing the version in the Balliol MS, as the choristers of The Queen's College, Oxford, still do late every December, as they lead the procession bearing the now rare dish.

> The bores hed in handis I brynge
> With garlondis gay and byrdis syngynge
> I pray you all helpe me to synge
> Que estis in convinio

The bores hed I understand
Yo cheffe serwyes in all this londe
Where so ever it may be fonde
Servitur eum sincfio

The bores hed I dare well say
Anon after the xⁱⁱth day
He taketh his leve and goth away
Exiunt tune di patria.

The reasons for the demise of the habit of eating a boar's head at Christmas are two. The first is a matter of taste, which Dorothy Hartley compares to 'cold boiled bacon, rather highly spiced'. (In fairness, though, I've tasted it myself, and brawn or normal French *charcutier*-made *fromage de tête* or *hure* is closer to the mark, which means you have to quite like crunchy and squishy bits of the pig as well as the meaty ones to enjoy it.) It is clear, though, from a passage found by J. A. R. Pimlott, that boar's head, at least in the form of brawn, was still an essential part of Christmas in 1745, when Thomas Gray wrote to Thomas Wharton, 'May you live a hundred Christ-masses and eat as many collars of brawn stuck with rosemary.'

The second and more dramatic reason is that the boar's head was a remnant of earlier, pre-Christian winter solstice celebrations. It was an all too fleshly link with paganism and the Norse gods, in particular. Its associations with the older religions go back almost as far as possible, even to the ancient Egyptian religion. In *The Golden Bough* Frazer has pages and pages on the sacredness and sacrifice of pigs, and on the twin poles of those eastern rites in which the pig was eaten and those, equal in number, in which eating pork was forbidden. The boar was certainly a sacred animal to many, and its sacrifice commemorated the death of Set, or Attis, or Adonis or Osiris. In short, the ritual killing of the boar was a substitute for the earlier rite in which a human being, a mock king, was sacrificed.

With the major exception of the Eucharist itself and the minor one of hot cross buns, Anglophone Christianity does not have many symbolic foods associated with its festivals. When you think about the practices of other religions in this regard, this seems a little surprising. At the Indian winter festival of Dewali, earthenware lamps are lit to show that, like Christmas and Hanukkah, this is a feast of light, sweetmeats are eaten and given as gifts. This profusion of sweets represents riches and wealth, for it is the festival of Lakshmi, goddess of wealth.

Jewish festivals are surrounded with symbolic food. At Purim, the feast of lots, observant Jews cele-brate the defeat by Queen Esther of Haman's plans to annihilate the Jewish people by eating pastries baked in the shape of Haman's three-cornered hat. At the Passover, the original of the Last Supper, the celebration of which is itself a meal, Jews eat bitter herbs to remind them of their ancestors' slavery in Egypt, salt water to recall their tears, a mixture of nuts and apple representing the mortar used in their labours, and various other food and drink designed to remind the participants in the *seder* meal of the ten plagues that descended upon the Egyptians and the sparing of the Jews; above all, water-biscuit-like *matzo* is eaten, because the haste of the exodus meant there was no time for leavened bread to be baked. At the New Year, apples and honey are eaten in the hope that the year to come will prove as sweet as the food, and even the Sabbath meal, eaten by definition once a week, has its symbolic bread and wine, and a chicken or some other symbol of plenty – if not luxury.

At Hanukkah the symbolism of the food is even more straightforward. It must be cooked in oil, to celebrate the miracle of the single day's supply of holy oil that lasted for eight days. In eastern Europe, and in the English-speaking countries to which Ashkenazi Jews emigrated, the Hanukkah food is, in Yiddish, the latke, or *levivot* in Hebrew, the potato pancake (see page 118). It is made exactly as the potato *crêpe* of eastern France, or that of Germany or Switzerland, with coarsely grated potato, onion, egg, some starchy binder (matzo meal usually, but sometimes plain flour), salt and pepper, and sometimes a rising agent such as baking powder. Formerly latkes were fried in the saturated rendered chicken, duck or goose fat that has contributed so much to the heartburn folklore of Jewish cooking and shortened so many Jewish lives. Nowadays they are more commonly, healthily and accurately fried in vegetable oil.

The major question, really, is how the potato got from Peru to the latke. In *Why We Eat What We Eat* Raymond Sokolov dates the first encounter of Europeans with the potato in 1537 in northern Peru, and reckons it reached Europe only in the 1570s and was first cultivated in Seville. The story that Sir Walter Raleigh brought the first spud to England from Virginia seems just plain wrong, though Tom Stobart says he grew a not very useful sort of potato on his Irish estate at Youghal, County Cork. It soon spread to Italy, and by 1739 was being grown extensively in Scotland though the French (and some other Western Europeans) were notoriously reluctant to eat it until it was popularised by Parmentier (1737–1818, whose name on a dish indicates the inclusion of potatoes in it). Irish immigrants took the potato back to America with them in 1719.

Sokolov has established that the chipped potato (or French fry) reached England around 1870 and that the potato chip (*anglice* crisp) recipe was published in America precisely in 1878. While that doesn't entirely sort out the latke situation, we are on safe ground, I think, in presuming potato cakes to have existed at least 50 years earlier. They seem to have originated in Russia, where, according to Faye Levy's *International Jewish Cookbook* (1992), Jews make latkes from all sorts of ingredients other than potatoes. She lists cheese, buckwheat flour and noodles.

The Russians had certainly worked out how to distil a liquor made from fermented potatoes, and by 1845 when the blight struck, the Irish had discovered most of the other uses to which the spud could be put. As the latke has several Irish cousins, you would think 1800 would be a reasonably conservative date for the first latke. Having said that, though, *The Jewish Manual* published in London 1846 and attributed to Lady Montefiore, and generally accepted as the first Jewish cookery book in English, has no recipe for latkes or any other Hanukkah food; the same is true of the *Jewish Cookery Book* by Mrs Esther Levy, published in Philadelphia in 1871, though she does give a recipe for potato fritters. They are, however, made from cooked potatoes and are sweet. Worse,

Edouard de Pomiane's *The Jews of Poland: Recollections and Recipes* (first published as *Cuisine Juive: Ghettos Modernes*, 1929) has the recipe, which uses virtually the same ingredients, for potato *kugel*, but none for latkes. This is a little disturbing, because it suggests that the tradition of latkes for Hanukkah may be of relatively recent origin. Or, to put it another way, as Raymond Sokolov does in another of his books, *The Jewish-American Kitchen*, 'since there were no potatoes available to any Jewish cook until the Spanish Conquest of Peru, some 1700 years later' than the re-dedication of the Temple by Judas Maccabaeus in 165BC, 'it is definitely the oil that connects these tasty pancakes to Hanukkah'.

Sephardic Jews may just have an older tradition. Israel has adopted the Sephardic habit, now catching on in north London Jewish communities as well, of eating jam doughnuts, *pontchikes* or *ponchkiss*, at Hanukkah. This has been brilliantly documented by Nicholas Stavroulakis in his *Cookbook of the Jews of Greece* (1990) in which he points out that 'as the sentiments of Hanukkah are overtly anti-Hellenist, and as the Hellenised Jews who settled in Greece would hardly celebrate what was in fact their own defeat, it is not surprising that Hanukkah is not a major holiday in Greece as it is in the West. In addition,' he says interestingly, 'Hanukkah's proximity to Christmas might account for the stress placed on a Jewish festival in Western countries. In Greece Christmas has become a major holiday only in recent years.'

The chief Hanukkah food eaten in Greece is called *zvingous*, a version of what are called *boumwelos* or *bimwelos* in Ladino, the vernacular of the Sephardic Jews. They are fried balls of choux pastry, unless made with milk, when they are called *loukoumades*. In America they are called doughnut holes, because they look like the bit missing from the centre of the doughnut shape. The frying medium is, of course, olive oil, and this particular food is common to all Sephardim. Greek Jews, however, have one of the largest repertoires of Hanukkah foods, including *tiganites*, pancakes flavoured with ouzo, masticha or raki, served sprinkled with cinnamon and sugar or honey and ground walnuts, or a whole wheat version called *lalangites* by the children of Ioannina at the turn of the century. In Corfu and Zakynthos *tiganites* are made of rice flour, as are the slightly different *fritoles*. And in Salonika and Hania, types of halva are eaten at Hanukkah, though these alone of Hanukkah treats are not fried foods.

There is a confused medieval folk tradition that assimilates the Apocryphal story of Judith with Hanukkah. In it Judith is a Hasmonean princess who serves a salt-preserved cheese to the Greek commander. He then drinks too much wine and, in his stupor, she beheads him and saves the kingdom. Some say that cheese dishes are eaten at Hanukkah because of this. The general point is clear, though; like most of the Jewish festival foods, and unlike most Western Christmas foods, Hanukkah foods are all symbolic.

Moreover, there are other reasons for the association of the holiday with fat or oil. In the eastern Mediterranean Hanukkah comes near the end of the olive harvest, just as the oil is being pressed. It also coincides with the end of the fattening season for geese, so that Jewish kitchens would be occupied with rendering the fat to preserve it for future use. Above

The boar's head, 1855

all, though, as Oded Schwartz points out in *In Search of Plenty* (1992), a history of Jewish food, the association of Hanukkah 'with oil and light is probably very old and belongs to a pagan ritual of fire and lights for warding off the approach of winter darkness'.

TO RETURN TO THE BOAR'S HEAD. WHEN DOROTHY Hartley published *Food in England* in 1954, she could still say: '"Ye Olde boar's head" may be bought, handsomely prepared, at provision stores in the Christmas season.' I have a dim memory of having seen, one Christmas, an elaborately confected tusker in the window of Richards, the pork butcher, in Oxford's covered market, but I think it was there for show, rather than for sale. Miss Hartley thought that if it was made from a wild boar it was 'always justifiably expensive' but that made from a domesticated pig was homely peasant fare. She actually tells how to make it, warning that it is a lot of trouble, though it 'makes a very imposing dish at very small cost'.

To sum up the fairly grisly recipe, you get the butcher to prepare the head, splitting it into two halves, joined only by the skin at the top. (Jane Grigson's recipe for *hure* starts in the same way.) 'Eyes, ears, snout and all the bone at the back should be removed,' says Miss Harley, 'and the brains wrapped separately.' You then pickle the head in saltpetre, salt and spices for a week or ten days and cook it by boiling gently in vegetables and flavourings until the bones are loose, and truss it, with the skinned tongue, into a conical shape. Ears and snout go to make up a gelatinous glaze; when the cone-shaped head is cold, it is brushed with this jelly, though, for some reason, the last coating must be poured over the pig's head.

'Serve "hym",' says Miss Hartley, 'on a convenient carving board, laid on a clean, flat fir bough.' She suggests giving 'hym' split almond tusks, prunes for eyes and a necklace of holly. You carve it lengthwise and serve it with mustard sauce; she repeats for emphasis that it is a 'very savoury form of cold spiced bacon', which will come as a disappointment to anyone who imagined that the object carried in with such ceremony was steaming hot. André Simon gives a recipe for pig's head in imitation of boar's head, which involves leaving the ears and snout in place – I think, but he is not explicit about this. He is quoting Alexis Soyer's recipe, which is for an actual wild boar, and makes everything clear by ending: 'Have some very fresh tulips and roses, which stick tastefully in the ears, and some around, but leaving space to carve.' If you ever feel ambitious enough to attempt a boar's head, do use the recipe in Jane Grigson's *Charcuterie*, which though a labour for giants, does at least give quantities and measures.

From the cook's point of view, it was a happy day when, because of the influence of churchmen or just because it became fashionable to have a hot main course for Christmas, roast goose took over from the boar's head. The boar's head may look spectacular, but so can the goose; and the goose definitely does not taste merely of cold bacon. There is a passage in Zola's *L'Assommoir* in which the appearance of the goose upon the table, 'huge, golden and flowing with its own juices' reduced everyone to silence: 'We didn't attack it immediately. There was a wonderment, a respectful surprise', while everyone at the table simply looked at the bird.

Dickens summed up the real pleasure of the Christmas goose: 'There never was such a goose. Bob said he didn't believe there ever was such a goose cooked. Its tenderness and flavour, size and cheapness were the themes of universal admiration. Eked out by apple-sauce and mashed potatoes, it was a sufficient dinner for the whole family; indeed, as Mrs Cratchit said with great delight (surveying one small atom of a bone upon the dish), "they hadn't ate it all at last!" Yet every one had had enough, and the youngest Cratchits in particular were steeped in sage and onion to the eyebrows.'

Though the golden days of the goose are probably in the past, the bird is increasingly available at Christmas, even in the supermarkets in Britain and France, and specialist growers do far more business at this time of year than before Michaelmas, whatever Dr Kitchiner thought about the proper season of the goose. Tom Stobart, by the way, disagrees with Dr Kitchiner anyway, and thinks that the goose is at his best 'from the autumn through to February'.

Game, on the other hand, is in season at Christmas, with the exception of grouse, whose season ends on December 10 because it began, along with that for snipe, way back on the Glorious Twelfth of August. Partridge and woodcock may be shot until the first of February, pheasant until the day before that, and furred game until April 30 when the shooting of red deer stops. The tradition of eating game at Christmas goes back to the days of sewing the roasted peacock back in its own skin and feathers, and to the one-bird-stuffed-inside-another Christmas pies of the last chapter. While it is difficult to make much of a dramatic statement with game, in the absence of peacocks it is a very good solution to the problem of variety, if there are not too many people around the Christmas board.

In recent years, in England, anyway, the price of pheasant in particular has fallen so greatly that it is feasible to cook it for a large number. The only difficulty is that an oven capable of roasting a large turkey does not find it so easy to cope with the same weight of smaller birds, so it can be tricky to roast pheasants for large numbers of people. (Though pheasant being so much richer, the quantity needed for a single serving is less than of turkey.) One year Frances Bissell and I dealt with this small crux by using only the breast of the pheasant, which we marinaded the day before in pomegranate juice and seeds, and grilled while the guests were eating the earlier courses (see page 122). It was very successful.

With all birds, wild or domesticated, the stuffing question is bound to arise. For many people, the stuffing is more of a treat than the birds; especially when the bird is turkey. Oddly enough, years of experiment have convinced me that the bird is always moister when it is *not* stuffed. Pop a citrus fruit, anything from a kumquat to a grapefruit, or an apple into the cavity, which you have salted and peppered, along with an onion, peeled or not, as you fancy, or some cloves of garlic, and you will have added to the flavour and moistness of the bird. The point is a simple one, really: the cooking juices either run into the stuffing, or back into the flesh of the fowl. You can achieve some very interesting flavouring combinations if you are willing to forgo stuffing the bird and fill the cavity instead with things such as chilli, fresh limes and slices of ginger; or an orange and a sprig of rosemary; or thyme, bay leaves and garlic; or tarragon and a lump of butter; or rub the cavity with light soya sauce, and insert ginger, garlic and spring onions, or with Thai *nam pla* and use garlic, chilli, ginger or galangal and bruised, sliced lemon grass. Even game birds benefit from garlic, thyme and juniper berries, or a chunk of German *Speck* or French *petit salé*, preferably blanched before inserting it into the bird's belly.

Part-cooked *boudin*, either black or white, makes a wonderful unorthodox stuffing for pheasant or chicken, as do *petit suisse* cheeses. Both give off moisture rather than absorbing it. The same moisturising effect is achieved by using any fatty sausage or meat, from minced beef or pork to steak.

You can, of course, stuff a bird with anything, and good rules to follow are something starchy for comfort, something aromatic for flavour, something crunchy for contrast, and maybe something meaty for luxury because it's Christmas. The starch can be anything from cooked potatoes to stale bread, but couscous, cooked rice and buckwheat can be used to add new interest. Aromatics: I think members of the onion family are essential for their perfume; whole heads of garlic, blanched, have quite a different flavour to single garlic cloves, and are suitable if the bird is going to cook slowly for a long time. The crunch can come from celery or from nuts; I'm partial to both in a stuffing, and both can be useful for keeping the texture of a farce loose and open. The bird's own liver is usually a delicious addition to a forcemeat, and some people insist on a Christmas stuffing having minced veal or sausage. You may be happier, though, with the extra flavour imparted by a bit of chopped ham, or the extra unctuousness conferred upon a stuffing by fat bacon.

Or you could always eat the ham on its own and forget about the bird altogether. There is a good deal to be said in favour of this, for as Xavier Aubryet said in *La Cuisinière Poétique* (1877), 'The pig is simply a vast dish walking around until it is time to be served up at table. His pink skin, spotted with black, brings to mind a truffled galantine; his firm and well-padded rump is already in the shape of a ham.' A whole ham is a noble sight; it has the drama necessary to be the centre of a celebration meal. When served hot, the best hams have a melting succulence; when cold, enough flavour to provide the perfect gastronomic foil for pickles, chutneys and interesting salads. It is our habit to have a ham on Boxing Day, the feast of St Stephen, December 26, an adjunct to Christmas totally lacking in the otherwise satisfactory celebrations of both the French and the Americans.

Ham, a common main course for Easter lunch in Britain, often takes pride of place on the American Christmas table. Because the turkey is *de rigueur* for Thanksgiving, which is the last Thursday in November, many American families have had enough turkey to last them for the month until Christmas, especially in the south, where the regional 'country' hams are so good. The best known are Kentucky and Virginia hams. These appellations mean a little more than the '*jambon de Paris* and *jambon d'York*' that are ubiquitous in France, and indicate not the place, but the style of the cure.

Virginia hams should come from the razorback breed of hog, and these should be fed on peanuts and peaches. Cured over fires of apple and hickory wood

Mutton hams being cured at Ashdown Smokers

and kept in old-fashioned smokehouses until ready, this ham is much less common than the poor quality western soft pork ham that has usurped its name by being cured commercially in Virginia. Smithfield hams are something else again; the name comes from a small town in Virginia, and not from the old

KEN HOM'S SINGAPORE-STYLE LETTUCE FRIED RICE

To go with Ken Hom's Christmas Roast Duck (see page 128), or on its own for supper after a lunch of too much turkey.

Serves 4

5–6 Chinese dried mushrooms
2 Tbsp peanut oil
4 shallots, sliced
3 cloves garlic, crushed
long-grain rice to the 400 ml (15 fl oz, scant 2 cups) level in a measuring jug, then cooked in the normal way
50 g (2 oz, ¼ cup) fresh or frozen peas
3 Tbsp finely minced spring onions
2 fresh chillies
2 eggs, beaten lightly
3 Tbsp light soy sauce
½ tsp salt
¼ tsp freshly ground black pepper
225 g (8 oz) iceberg lettuce, shredded
2 Tbsp finely chopped spring onions, as garnish

Soak the dried mushrooms in warm water for 20 mins, squeeze out liquid, discard stems and cut the caps into small dice.

Heat a wok or large frying pan and add the oil (after the wok is hot – this is important in Chinese cooking). When almost smoking add the shallots and garlic and stir-fry for 30 secs. Add the cold, cooked rice and stir-fry for 1 min; then add mushrooms, peas, spring onions and chillies (chopped if you want the dish to be hot; whole if you want only to flavour the dish, in which case, remove before serving). Continue to stir-fry for another 3 mins. Stir in the eggs, soy sauce, salt and pepper and stir-fry for a further 2 mins or until the eggs have set.

Finally add the lettuce and mix thoroughly. Turn out on to a warmed serving plate, garnish with the spring onions and serve at once.

THE EASIEST VEGETABLE RECIPE THERE IS

Take whatever member of the squash family is available – Turk's cap, butternut, patty pan, a small pumpkin – pierce it several times with a skewer or knife blade, and microwave it on full power until you can smell it. It's done. When you can handle it, cut it in half and discard the seeds, season and serve. Or scoop out the flesh into a gratin or soufflé dish and season with butter, cream, olive or nut oil, and sweet spices such as grated nutmeg, ground cinnamon or cardamom – or with ground cumin and coriander seed. Don't forget salt and pepper.

You can do this in a conventional oven as well, but you need to oil the skin of the squash, and open the oven door from time to time for a good sniff.

FRANCES BISSELL'S WILD RICE WITH WILD MUSHROOMS

Cook the wild rice according to the directions on the packet using three volumes of liquid, either lightly salted water or stock, to one of rice. Check its progress. Some people like it with a little crunch left, others prefer it when each grain has exploded fully.

Clean and slice whatever wild mushrooms you can acquire. Ceps are wonderful, so are golden *girolles* and black *trompettes de la mort; pieds de mouton* are fine, and oyster mushrooms will do when there's nothing more interesting. They can all be supplemented with good cultivated mushrooms, and sometimes the chestnut-coloured ones have more flavour than some in the list above. I shouldn't bother with fresh shiitake mushrooms, but reconstituted dried ones are excellent.

Sauté the mushrooms apart from the rice, in olive oil, butter or a mixture of both, with or without some diced onion, shallot or garlic, as the mood takes you. Combine this with the cooked rice and serve with a generous dusting of minced parsley or green coriander.

KEN HOM'S RED-COOKED WINTER VEGETABLES

With the duck and the Lettuce Fried Rice (see pages 128 and 132), plus a light dessert, this would make a complete Chinese-style Christmas dinner, but it can be served Western-style and will go well with a spicy white wine or a young, fruity red.

Red-cooking is a technique usually employed for cooking meats, simmering them in a rich, red sauce of Chinese spices, and you can easily adapt the recipe for meat, poultry or even a very sturdy fish. Ken Hom discovered, though, that it works equally well with vegetables, making a quick, tasty stew. You might like this after the Christmas binge, with a bit of grilled chicken or meat, and a green salad.

Serves 4
450 g (1 lb) carrots
225 g (8 oz) turnips
1 Tbsp peanut oil
2 cloves garlic, peeled and crushed with a knife (not in a garlic press)
2 tsp coarsely chopped fresh root ginger
2 Tbsp hoisin sauce
1 Tbsp dark soy sauce
2 tsp sugar
150 ml (5 fl oz) water

Peel and cut the carrots into 2.5-cm (1-in) pieces. Peel the turnips and cut into 2.5-cm (1-in) cubes. Heat a wok or large frying pan. Add the oil, then the garlic and ginger. Stir-fry for 10 secs and add the carrots, hoisin sauce, soy sauce, sugar and water. Cover and cook over high heat for 8 mins. Then add the turnips and cook for another 3 mins or until the vegetables are tender but not mushy. There will be very little sauce left. Turn on to a hot platter and serve.

BAKED BEETROOT

Take fresh, scrubbed but not peeled beetroots and put them in a double thickness of foil, with as many cloves of peeled garlic as you like. Add salt and pepper and drizzle over olive oil. Seal the foil parcel loosely, and cook exactly as you would bake a potato. It's done when it gives a little to the touch, or a skewer goes in easily. Peel the beetroot while still it is warm, slice and eat with the golden-brown garlic. Or dress with olive oil, a squeeze of lemon and salt and pepper, scatter the garlic about with some chopped parsley or chives, and eat at room temperature as a salad or first course.

cheeses won the Supreme Championship and several other prizes at the Nantwich Show in 1980, the last time the cheeses of this region have been judged on such a grand scale.

Most farmhouse cheshire is now matured in wax, which coats the natural cloth binding. This is deplored by Lance Appleby, none of whose cheeses is waxed; and Rance says his opposition to waxing ought to give pause for thought to the other producers. Appleby is convinced that waxed cheeses tend to sweat, says Rance, 'a long-standing worry of cheshire cheesemakers ... Most cheeses are now waxed and graded for eating young, a deprivation for lovers of mature rich cheshire.' Count me in. That is why we try to buy a small truckle of Appleby's cheshire and mature it ourselves – a simple matter of standing it in a cool, dry, well-ventilated place and remembering to turn it at least once a week.

Note that Major Rance warns that 'genuine farmhouse cheshires are stamped with the number of the farm, together with the date of making and "superfine" or "fine" grading. Waxed cheeses not so marked may not be sold as farmhouse Cheshire.' The Appleby's number is 125.

There has been an almost more remarkable renaissance of farmhouse cheesemaking in Ireland, which is not restricted to traditional varieties, but includes many cheeses that have analogues in France, such as blue cheeses and washed-rind cheeses. If you see Milleens, Gubbeen or Cashel Blue, buy it. In America, it is very worthwhile experimenting with the new cheeses made in the Pacific Northwest; I sampled some sensational examples being sold in Seattle. There are also a large number of goat cheeses made by artisans

The cheese fair at Islington Dairy Show, October 8, 1878

in Britain and Ireland, though I have never tasted any so good as those made by Laurie Chenel in California. But goat cheese is not at its best at Christmas, so we don't include it on our cheeseboard. Its season is April to October, and beware of buying any later than November. There should be no fresh milk available then, as the nanny goat's kids should be taking it all.

Red wine is not always better with cheese than

white wine. In fact, some cheeses savage red wine. Stilton is a good example, for almost all blue cheeses are temperamental in this regard. It is famously well known that the best combination of wine and cheese is sauternes and roquefort; but several other white wines, including all the *viognier*-based ones of the Rhône, and many of the wines from Alsace, stand up well to roquefort's aggression. Few reds survive the encounter at all; though one of our strange findings in our tastings was that Bouzy rouge, the red version of the pinot noir usually vinified white for blending in champagne, is superb with roquefort.

All these whites are better with stilton than most reds, though we found some merit in matching it with powerful older rhônes. It will not do any favours for the claret or for fuller red burgundies, though light, fruity pinot noir comes out of the conflict relatively unscathed, which points to a pinot noir d'Alsace, perhaps, or a red Sancerre. Best of all, though, is the Englishman's traditional answer to what to drink with stilton: port. Vintage port usually has the guts to deal with the cheese bully; but I think I prefer the nuttiness of an older tawny. One year we had some Taylor's Twenty-Year-Old Tawny with the Colston Bassett. I can still remember the combination.

Port is also glorious with the cheddar and the cheshire, as it is with the vacherin, if you happen to have any to hand. It is with the hard English cheeses, though, that good claret and burgundy come into their own. The wine is flattered by the cheese (as claret, especially, is by old Gouda — look out for three-year-old, if you've got a bottle of great claret to show off); the rich, warm flavours of mature cheese are brought out by good red wine.

FROMAGE FRAIS AUX HERBES

Sometimes, either because you feel you've binged, or because you need to eat something that reminds you of summer, you want a really light dish after Christmas, on Boxing Day or New Year's Day. Buy a carton or two of *fromage frais*, which comes with percentages of butterfat from zero to slightly, but not very, rich. Whisk it with a fork and incorporate whatever chopped fresh herbs you can find. Chives are the most desirable but most rare at that time of year, so use the green tops of spring onions sliced terribly finely. Add a bit of minced garlic, salt and pepper, and stir in a drizzle of the fruitiest olive oil you can find.

If the mixture is not stiff enough to stand up on its own (possibly because you've used 0 per cent butterfat) either serve it as a dip with crudités, or mix in enough low-fat cottage cheese to give it the consistency that allows you to eat it with a fork. Served, for example, with a tomato salad made simply by slicing good tomatoes thickly stem-end down, salted and peppered (and sugared if their flavour is insipid), with oil and no vinegar, scattered with herbs including basil if possible, it will give you the illusion of having lunch on the beach somewhere in the Mediterranean.

CHAPTER SEVEN

The sweet conclusion

It is only yesterday, as it were, since the traditional ending to the Christmas feast has become a flaming plum pudding, decorated with a sprig of holly, and containing a silver coin and other charms hidden within its hemispherical shape. From Tudor and Stuart times, right down to the Edwardian era, the Christmas pudding was only one among many of the sweet conclusions to the great spread. Nowadays, instead of having a table laden with flavoured creams, fruit jellies and light, frothy puddings, we have a single plum pudding (which, though it has a good deal of dried fruit, may contain no plums at all), served with hard sauce or brandy butter. If Christmas dinner is served at lunchtime, in Britain at least, this is likely to be followed, at all too short an interval, by mince pies served at tea-time, accompanied by Christmas cake, an all-too-rich fruitcake encased in a layer of marzipan under a shell of rock-hard royal icing adorned with a sprig of holly.

America is not addicted to Christmas pudding, and the French, on the whole, shudder at the thought of it, while adhering loyally to their sticky, rich, often gooey chocolate *bûche de Noël*. I was astonished, when doing the research for the television programme associated with this book, to discover several shops in Boulogne that sold *le plum pouding*. It transpired on close questioning that it is not the taste of the residents of the Pas de Calais for steamed puddings that is responsible for its presence in these shops, so much as their proximity to the English Channel. On the whole, the French attitude to this apparently medieval dish is to say that, as a nation, they have also lost their taste for feudalism, *droit de seigneur* and eating with the hands from wooden trenchers. More about the medieval aspect in a moment.

One firm, Matthew Walker of Derby, manufactures almost 40 per cent of the Christmas puddings eaten in the world, including virtually all those sold under their own labels by the British supermarkets. There are 120 different recipes currently in production, so each product is genuinely different from each of the others. Still, for Christmas 1992 they hoped to sell 8 million puddings. Incidentally, the French market has trebled in size recently. It could just be that this is accounted for entirely by British expatriates buying them at Fauchon in Paris; but I suspect the existence of a French underground of plum-pudding eaters.

Let us note that in some parts of America, particularly the south, though plum pudding is seldom on the Yule menu, nut-laden fruitcake, heavily laced with spirits, often is. At Thanksgiving, Americans have a prescribed dessert in pumpkin pie; but just as Christmas is the less important feast in the United States, so the rules for making up the meal are more relaxed.

Not only the ingredients and method of cooking, but the very ritual of making the Christmas pudding seems antique. Stir-up Sunday, the first Sunday before Advent, which is itself the Sunday before St Andrew's day, is when, by tradition, the whole family gathers around the mixing bowl. Each member from youngest to oldest stirs from east to west in commemoration of the journey of the Magi in the same direction, while silently making a wish. Though this could easily be a custom stretching back to 1066 and beyond, it actually originated in the 19th century.

Indeed, it is only since 1836 that plum pudding has been called 'Christmas' pudding, says Maggie Black in her finely researched Women's Institute *Calendar of Feasts* (1985, reprinted in Davidson's *On Fasting & Feasting*). Though George I had a plum pudding on his first Christmas in England in 1714, it was not then a dish exclusively associated with Christmas. Indeed, over a hundred years later, William IV had a plum pudding to celebrate his birthday.

It is commonly known that our modern, solid Christmas pudding originated in a thick liquid dish; what is startling is that the solid version and the more primitive liquid one co-existed for over two hundred years. The first reference to a solid Christmas pudding, a recipe only recently published, is as early as 1604; the latest recipe for a liquid one seems to be 1841.

Christmas porridge or broth sounds very odd to modern ears and not very attractive to modern palates. (The terms 'Christmas porridge' and 'plum porridge', 'Christmas broth' and 'plum broth' and 'Christmas pottage' or 'plum pottage' are all interchangeable.) But many Scandinavians even today eat a sweetened rice porridge as their Christmas Eve first course, which was also the position in the meal occupied by the British Christmas porridge. The hardship of a meal begun in this way is mitigated by the fact that a charm – a blanched almond – is hidden in the rice pudding, and its recipient gets a present.

Though a recent article in the press (in the *Observer*, 22 December 1991) repeats the old saw that the Christmas pudding 'is said to be derived from the time of William the Conqueror, when it consisted of a thick soup containing beef, raisins, currants, bread and suet', the first trace of the recipe, says C. Anne Wilson in *Food and Drink in Britain* (1973), is actually in the early 15th century, when it was called 'stewet beef to potage'. The recipe then had chunks of beef seethed in water and a lot of wine with minced onion, herbs, bread for thickening, a red colouring agent, seasonings of cloves, cinnamon and mace and, most importantly, currants. The point about this recipe, which was not then especially associated with Christmas, is that it is one of the few of many meat and dried fruit pottages of its type that survived into Georgian times, by which era most 'such compositions had lost their appeal and were rarely eaten', according to Anne Wilson.

In its Elizabethan version it acquired prunes, along with the raisins and currants. The prunes, a Tudor touch, were imported; they had already been added to meat pies, but were only now added to stews. They made such an impact on Tudor cooks that, says Anne Wilson, the name 'subsequently became a token of the other dried fruits; so that plum cake and plum porridge were confections containing some dried fruits, but not necessarily prunes'. In *English Bread and Yeast Cookery* Elizabeth David made the same point about figs, as well. 'Figgy' pudding very often contained raisins and currants, but no figs. By the time of Gervase Markham's 1615 *The English House-Wife*, his 'ordinary stewed broth' had lost its herbs but was otherwise identical. Then by 1660, with the publication of Robert May's *The Accomplisht Cook*, it had become a celebratory dish appropriate – still as a first course – for All Saints', Christmas and New Year's Day. Finally, by 1673, William Rabisha first called it a special Christmas dish, and soon after it was commonly called Christmas broth or Christmas or plum porridge. It was most often spiked with alcohol – claret and sack are the most frequently mentioned sorts – and could be made in advance and stored in earthenware pots. So the question of whether it's a medieval dish depends on what view you take of when the Renaissance started in England.

Along with mince pies, plum porridge became a particular horror to the Puritans in their campaign against Christmas. J. A. R. Pimlott quotes an anonymous rhymester of the 17th century saying, 'Plum broth was Popish, and mincepie – oh, that was sheer idolatry', and Sir Thomas Overbury caricatured a Puritan who attacked the Pope by refusing to eat the Christmas broth he was offered. Curiously, the heirs of the Puritans, the Dissenters, also bore plum porridge a grudge. Sir Roger de Coverly expressed surprise and pleasure that a strict Dissenter who had Christmas dinner at his house ate up his serving of plum porridge.

'When exactly plum pudding ousted plum porridge is a mystery,' wrote Mr Pimlott in 1978, 'which it must be left to later research to resolve.' The strange answer, as hinted at the beginning of this chapter, is, in historical terms, the day before yesterday. Pimlott himself quotes several authorities that appear to show that Christmas broth reigned supreme during the 18th century: '"Everyone from the King to the artisan eats soup and Christmas pies," wrote de Saussure in 1726. "The soup is called Christmas-porridge, and is a dish few foreigners find to their taste."' In David Garrick's 1774 *Christmas Tale* he says that it is indigestible to the foreign palate. An earlier reference is the Rev. W. Vickers writing to his correspondent in 1717 that, 'We can't come up to your country fare plumb porrage, but must be content with onions and garlic.'

Writers of recipes also confirm the position of plum porridge in the 18th century. Hannah Glasse's 1747 *The Art of Cookery* gives 'Plumb-Porridge for Christmas': 'Make a beef broth with 8 gallons of water', the recipe begins, and continues with the familiar bread, prunes, raisins, currants, wine and spices. Hannah Glasse also has a 'boiled plumb pudding', but it has no connection with Christmas, and is less rich than her plum porridge. Even so, it is recognisably related to our own plum pudding, as it's made from suet, breadcrumbs, eggs, currants, raisins, nutmeg and ginger. Though there's an ambiguity about the date in his text, Pimlott seems to think that by the end of the 18th century 'an unnoticed revolution had taken place, and the plum-pudding had almost universally replaced its odd predecessor on the Christmas table'.

He cites in support of this a Mr Brand, who ate plum porridge at a dinner with the royal chaplains in

153

1801, and remarked that he did not know that it was still eaten. Even so, Pimlott found an exception. In 1841 Benson E. Hill's *Epicure's Almanac*, says Pimlott, 'gave recipes for both dishes, with the interesting difference that the porridge was to be made on 22 December and the pudding on Christmas Eve.' This must be the last such recipe, for the latest Anne Wilson found was Margaret Dods in 1826 who cited it as a Scottish recipe. Perhaps, says Anne Wilson, 'it lingered longer in Scotland than in other parts of Britain. Elsewhere the meatless plum pudding had already prevailed.'

We can agree that the porridge still hadn't quite disappeared by the mid-19th century. What is odder is that Hilary Spurling has found a recipe for the solid pudding that is earlier than anyone suspected. Lady Fettiplace (c.1570–c.1647) lived in an age that was a small time-pocket of female literacy. Under the influence of the Queen herself, well-bred girls learned to read and write for a brief period of 20 years or so. By the time of Elinor Fettiplace's death, under the Commonwealth, female literacy was once again discouraged. It is our good luck that Lady Fettiplace seems in 1604 to have written down a number of her own recipes. Mrs Spurling has published these as *Elinor Fettiplace's Receipt Book* (1986), where she says: 'We tend to think of Christmas pudding as a Victorian speciality, if not a 19th-century invention, but Lady Fettiplace made hers from virtually the same ingredients – eggs, breadcrumbs, suet, dried fruit and spices – in the same hospitable quantities as Mrs Beeton.' Mrs Spurling has told me that though the recipe is not explicitly linked to Christmas (none of Lady Fettiplace's recipes has any commentary attached to it), she is convinced that it was meant for use at Christmas, especially since the Christmas festivities in Lady Fettiplace's household went from November to Twelfth Night, and the pudding is clearly a midwinter dish.

The recipe must, of course, have been current and used in this form or another by hundreds or even thousands of Elizabethan cooks. The difference is that Lady Fettiplace could write it down. Her pudding is cooked in a sheep's paunch, like a haggis. It says: 'Take twelve eggs & breake them, then take crumbs of bred, & mace & currance & dates cut small, & some oxe suet small minced & some saffron, put all these in a sheepes Mawe, & so boile it.' Mrs Spurling glosses this as 2 lb (1 kg) of breadcrumbs and of suet, 5–6 lb (about 2½ kg) of dried fruit and 8–10 hours of boiling. As she points out, interpolating the quantities from Dorothy Hartley's recipe, which is said to be that used by the royal family since the days of George I, Lady Fettiplace's recipe would feed anywhere from 40 to 56 people. The saffron is an unusual ingredient, and makes one think of much older, properly medieval dishes.

In 1604 the pudding had to be boiled in an animal's stomach because, says Maggie Black, the pudding cloth was only invented in 1617. She thinks that the porridge mixture got richer and thicker until it became a candidate for boiling in a bag or cloth, but, as we have seen, the eggy pudding had already existed for at least a decade. I suspect, in fact, that it's a very great deal older than that – perhaps even as old as the porridge. But cleaning an animal's paunch was just as messy a job in the Middle Ages as it is today and, until the pudding cloth was invented, it must

The Cavalier is toasting not the Christmas pudding, but Margery, who is carrying it

it. By 1816 Dr William Kitchiner, says Maggie Black, had created a plum pudding with brandy as a (one imagines unorthodox) Lenten dish and the circle was complete: the solid pudding had become associated with Christmas and then moved away again to become a dish associated with feasting in general.

As Maggie Black astutely observes, the Christmas pudding was a unifying dish, a democratic dish. As it 'could be boiled in a pot over the family fire', it was economical with fuel, and its relatively inexpensive ingredients must have been a welcome supplement to many a 'poor man's usually meagre beef or goose. It was in this role,' Maggie Black continues, 'that Charles Dickens saw it. Good journalist that he was, he wrote it up as the central symbol of Christmas cheer and plenty, and found a receptive audience. The new urban middle class was seeking to recreate what they believed had been medieval Christmas revelry.'

Their belief wasn't quite accurate, as we've seen. But the Christmas pudding acquired its central position as the symbol of Christmas feasting by ousting another culinary rival. It took over and transformed the ingredients of the Christmas porridge, but it literally captured the charms of the Twelfth Night cake.

In my family we try to remember, but usually forget, to put a silver coin in the Christmas pudding before it gets its second boiling. (We save a no-longer-legal-tender silver sixpence for this purpose – other families still guard a silver threepenny piece – but, of course, can never remember where it is so carefully kept.) Some families actually insert in their Christmas pudding the full panoply of charms: a thimble whose recipient will remain a spinster, a button for a bachelor, a ring for a wedding, a tiny horseshoe bringing

have been far easier to serve porridge for Christmas than the more solid pudding. Even so, we shouldn't forget that the two dishes served different purposes – one was a first course, the other a final course.

The porridge had perhaps always had alcohol in it. The solid pudding did not, at least in Lady Fettiplace's version. The one served to George I, however, contained a large wine glass of brandy, and Mrs Maria Rundell's 1806 Common Plum Pudding had wine in

good luck, as well as the coin bringing good fortune. These tokens were transferred directly from another institution, the Twelfth Night cake, and their transference marked its demise in England. Naturally this shift could only be accomplished when Christmas pudding has assumed its solid form: porridge eaters would be in danger of choking on concealed charms.

The Twelfth Night cake has survived as a recipe in Britain, where it has become Christmas cake; and as an institution in France, though the recipe has changed utterly. We shall discuss the French Twelfth Night cake later.

The disappearance of the Twelfth Night cake began in the 1850s. Its demise was brought about by the change in attitude noted by the writer in an 1850 special Christmas supplement in the *Illustrated London News* (quoted in Bridget Ann Henisch *Cakes and Characters*, 1984, which is the definitive book on this subject). The writer pointed out the difference between the appearance of the grocer's shop on Christmas Eve and the confectioner's shop as Epiphany approaches: 'It is the first only which produces the real national excitement.' Whereas in the past the Twelfth Night cake would have been the centre of every kind of interest and appetite, its appeal is now 'confined to the sense of sight. Fine combinations of saccharine splendour for the eyes; Kings and Queens, ill-formed but gorgeously gilt and frosted for the eyes; pippin-paste involved into curious scrolls – all for the eyes. But the interest of the Grocer's Shop on Christmas Eve penetrates far more deeply into the soul of the surveying crowd. Many, many of them, far beyond the limits of twelfth-cake consumers, hope to share practically in the boiled luxury. While the twelfth-cake is a more aristocratic type, the plum-pudding is a national symbol.'

Here is the nub of the matter. Christmas pudding has become democratic: 'It does not represent a class or a caste, but the bulk of the English nation. There is not a man, woman, or child raised above what the French would call *prolétaires*, that does not expect to taste a plum-pudding of some sort or other on Christmas Day.'

What about the charms? Originally they bore a direct line of descent from Saturnalia, for they began as a single bean. Its recipient was the King of the Bean, the temporary Lord of Misrule, the Master of the Revels. Sometimes there was a pea concealed in the cake as well, and the lady who got it became Queen; sometimes the King awarded the pea to a lady of his choosing. The power of the bean and the pea as fertility symbols was not lost on the revellers.

Twelfth Night festivities were so important that Shakespeare as well as Ben Jonson and Inigo Jones drew on the traditions of the masque; Kings diced at their courts, and gambling was licensed where state lotteries were organised; Samuel Pepys gave a new-fangled Twelfth-Night party where people assumed theatrical roles in a charade dictated by stock characters written on slips of paper and drawn out of a hat; and Thackeray wrote a 'book of Twelfth Night characters'.

The evolution of the Christmas pudding charms, then, was from the original bean, via the character cards, which by Pepys's time were no longer strips of paper concealed in the cake but a separate pack. By the mid-19th century these were types such as 'Park's New Twelfth-Night Characters' and included the violent, knife-wielding and melancholy Dicky Daggerwood and Mrs Daggerando; the bolters, Mr Benjamin Bounce and Countess Fly Away; the dandy, Swellerando and the fashion plate, Lady Low Sleeve; the boring, pipe-smoking Lord Dumble Dum Dreary; Lord Flirt Away and Lady Languish; the musical Lady Warble and Madame Mandoline; and the dancers Georgie Galloppara and Fanny Fandango. You assumed the character of the name you drew, consulting the illustrations in the book, and played him or her in the charade established by the host or the Bean King.

The Christmas pudding charms represented a simplification of these characters, now reduced to the stereotypes of the Spinster, the Bachelor, the Bride, the Gambler and the Rich Man. In most households the charms long ago disappeared altogether except for the silver coin – and even that is usually wrapped in a tiny parcel of greaseproof paper to make it more difficult for the recipient to swallow it.

The French maintain the Epiphany cake tradition assiduously, bean and all. The antiquity of the ceremony of *tirer le roi*, or choosing the king, is shown by the fact that the bean is a *fève* or fava bean, the one bean that is of old world and not American origin. Nowadays the bean is often replaced by a china replica-bean, or by a teeny-tiny porcelain Baby Jesus, or by a metal charm meant to become part of a girl's bracelet after the cake has been consumed. I recently burnt my fingers on a miniature Les Invalides in a cake just out of the oven, part of a series of the *Monuments Historiques de Paris* designed for pâtissiers to bury in their *galettes de Rois*, as the French cakes are called, in honour of the three kings, the Magi.

The *galette* is now nearly always the Paris recipe with flaky pastry, though there are still a few regional differences in Twelfth-Night cakes. In Savoy they eat brioche or fruitcake and in Vervier it has cinnamon and sugar candy. Originally the Epiphany cake was made by the bakers, the *boulangers*. But the *pâtissiers* lobbied the French parliament on the grounds that the recipe used butter and eggs, and not just the ingredients of bread. The bakers won, though, and continued to sell Twelfth-Night cake right up to 1914. Now you usually find them for sale in the pastry shops, starting just after New Year's Day. They come with a gilded cardboard crown, to be worn by whoever finds the charm. As it is usually an occasion for having close friends to dinner, the custom has grown in some places that the person who is king one year must buy the cake (and usually the champagne, too) for the next year's celebration.

Twelfth Night had a reputation for excess. In *Simple French Food* Richard Olney quotes Prosper-Montagné citing a 17th-century tract condemning the debauchery of the period: 'Large groups gather (on the Twelfth-Night) to elect a king; he chooses his cabinet members and then the celebration begins, continuing for days with the festivities multiplying until all purses are empty and the creditors arrive.' 'Nowadays,' says Olney, 'the game is an innocent excuse for friends to gather together and drink a couple of bottles of Champagne; it is apparently still great fun, for hardly is everyone recovered from celebrating the advent of the New Year than people begin gathering to *tirer les Rois* and it goes on throughout the month of January, the person crowned being designated as the next to receive; quite distinguished company is apt to turn loud and bawdy in the joyous atmosphere.'

Returning to the Christmas meal itself, there is the practical problem that not everyone likes plum pudding, and while you feel you must have it, if only for the sake of tradition, it is nice to have something enjoyable to eat; otherwise the Christmas feast takes on some aspects of those rubber-chicken dinners politicians and charity workers are obliged to eat so often. At our house we have solved that by instituting an alternative tradition.

It was Claudia Roden's idea to have a Moroccan pastry 'snake' for Christmas lunch, and she always makes it herself, from her own recipe. It has some affinity for (and some of the same ingredients as) pastries such as the Christmas fish of Lecce, described by Patience Gray in her *Honey from a Weed* (1986). Most of all, it is a large and impressive confection, suitable for a feast, but made from ingredients most people like – almonds and filo pastry. It is scented with orange-flower or rosewater, which makes it reminiscent of dozens of English dishes dating back as far back as Richard II. Having the snake at our own table reminds us that English food at that time, as revealed by the recipes in the first cookery book in English, *A Forme of Cury*, was indistinguishable from much that is eaten, even now, in the Middle East. There is a similar recipe in Lady Fettiplace's book, for a breadcrumb-thickened almond pudding cooked in a sausage casing. Not only is the shape similar to the snake, but the flavour is the same combination of almonds and rosewater, which of course goes back to the Arabs.

Cooking with scents such as orange-flower water or rosewater was very common in the 16th- and early 17th-century English kitchen, presumably because of the connection with the Arabs that went back to the Crusades. But Hilary Spurling makes the very good point that though rosewater is used in a great many of Lady Fettiplace's recipes, it is a 'a self-effacing ingredient', its elusive scent and flavour scarcely noticeable in the strong-smelling and strong-tasting company it often keeps. She remarks that it is very often used as the basic moistening element in a recipe, and that it must therefore be employed in lieu of 'dubious, muddy, polluted, twice used' ordinary water, which nobody at the time would even have considered drinking. Rosewater was distilled, and whether bought or made at home, came in clean, stoppered jars.

So though it may appear idiosyncratic, our new practice of eating the 'snake' at Christmas has a sound historical grounding. Equally 'medieval', and much more authentically traditional at Christmas, is mincemeat. Christmas pie was always mincemeat, and though the mixture of meat and dried fruit sounds self-evidently medieval, mincemeat is first documented in the 16th century. Thomas Tusser puts mince or 'shred' pies on his 1557 list of foods that were standard at Christmas.

One of the most interesting discussions of mincemeat is in Hilary Spurling's edition of Lady Fettiplace's recipes. Elinor Fettiplace's quantities are unusually precise for the period, so one can get a very good idea of what her mince pies tasted like – and they are nothing at all like modern ones. 'They turned out,' says Mrs Spurling, 'to be in fact little savoury pies, rich and fruity but not at all sweet, and quite

'The glutton' by Thomas Rowlandson (1756–1827)

unsuited to tea time.' They are far from our ordinary mince tarts, and much more like samosas 'and other dry, mildly spiced meat pasties of the Middle East', or like Latin American *empanadas*. The fruit is used in equal quantities with the meat (boiled mutton in this case) and suet (beef suet is specified) and the sugar used is only twice as much as the salt, which of course gives a savoury balance. Indeed, sugar is here used, like salt, as only a seasoning. The other ingredients are orange peel, raisins, rosewater, ginger, mace, nutmeg and cinnamon.

This must have been one of the last such recipes to show such a strong Middle Eastern influence, as Gervase Markham's mince pies, only a dozen or so years later, contain no salt at all. Mrs Spurling points out that the proportion of sugar rose as the quantity of meat was reduced, until the present, when English mincemeat contains no meat at all. (In fact, says Mrs Spurling, modern English mincemeat recipes are greatly improved in texture by the addition of a little minced tongue, beef or mutton.)

A Frenchman, M. Henri Misson, a translation of whose memoirs of his travels in England was published in 1719, approved of English 'Christmass Pye', as he did not of most English food: 'It is a great Nostrum the Composition of this Pastry; it is a most learned Mixture of Neats-Tongues, Chicken, Eggs, Sugar, Raisins, Lemon and Orange Peel, various kinds of Spicery.' The recipe hasn't changed much in America, where it still contains meat, and the chief alteration to the British recipe is the addition of ardent spirits in place of Lady Fettiplace's distilled rosewater. Mrs Beeton's ordinary mincemeat recipe contains 1 lb (½ kg) of lean beef and a pint (generous ½ litre) of brandy, whereas her superior offering called 'Excellent Mincemeat' (see page 165) contains no meat and a larger proportion of brandy to suet and fruit. Mincemeat had acquired its alcohol at least by the time of Sir Kenelm Digby's 1668 recipe, which calls for a little sack or sherry.

The Puritans hated mince pies even more than they disliked plum porridge. The Puritan figure in the dramatist Fletcher's 1656 *Christmas Day* apostrophises the pie thus:

Idolatrie in crust! Babylon's whore
Rak'd from the grave, and bak'd by hanches,
    then
Sew'd up in Coffins to unholy men;
Defil'd, with superstition, like the Gentiles
Of old, that worship'd onions, roots and lentiles!

But the mince pie continued, as it does today, to be associated with Christmas. In England it was

159

regarded as an indigenous, unfancy food. In 1754 the *Connoisseur* decried what it found to be the recent neglect of the 'solid, substantial, Protestant mince-pie', which was as much a part of Christmas as pan-cake to Shrove Tuesday or goose to Michaelmas.

This was the tradition taken over by the American colonists, and accounts for the fact that the American recipes are food fossils, much less evolved than their British counterparts. This statement is true despite the rule-proving exception of James Beard, who put strawberry jam in his mincemeat (see page 164).

Like all the Christmas foods we have examined, neither Christmas broth, Christmas pudding, Christmas cake nor Christmas pie has any symbolic connection with the festival. They all have an historic reason for their association with the feast, but nothing that apparently reflects anything to do with the meaning of the celebration.

In parts of France, however, the final course is laden with significance. The 13 desserts of Provence stand for Jesus and the twelve Apostles, and even some of the foods that make it up have their own, individual meaning. The fruits, nuts, sweetmeats and pastries that compose the *treize desserts* are some-times not put out until the *réveillon* after the return from midnight mass; but they are always left on the table until Twelfth Night, and usually replenished as needed. The ingredients of course vary from place to place, and even from household to household. But they have in common that everyone tries to use as many foodstuffs as possible from the region itself, and this is always interpreted as narrowly as possible; so if your village has a special sweetmeat, for instance, its inclusion in the *treize desserts* is *de rigueur*.

Richard Olney thinks the whole Christmas Eve supper, of which this series of desserts is the conclusion, is a sort of Provençal Thanksgiving, which is why the dishes, like the 'lavish-sounding' desserts, are each chosen for 'its humble and homely character'.

It is not often remarked, but many of the fruits and nuts featured are common to the Mediterranean, and so are found in the Holy Land as well as Provence; and some of the sweetmeats have their counterparts in Middle Eastern confections. The essentials are the four 'beggars', the fruits and nuts representing the colours of the habits of the mendicant orders of friars. Thus white dried figs for the Franciscans, almonds for the Carmelites, hazelnuts for the Dominicans and black raisins for the Augustines. Fresh fruit comes, if possible, from your own property – which means saving some bunches of grapes if at all possible, though in most places it comes down to apples and pears. In the Vaucluse there is often melon, and the expensive whole candied melon that is the speciality of Aix-en-Provence is on the tables of those who can afford it. In the hill-villages of the Maures there are the chestnuts, the processing of which is one of the few local industries.

Tangerines, oranges and dates have always had to come from North Africa, though some of the citrus fruits will grow on the French Riviera. Almond-paste sweets called Calissons d'Aix are another expensive addition to the desserts; and many families still have the ritual of making their own nougat, by adding grilled almonds and bits of sugar to bubbling hot honey. It is invariably so hard that it has to be smashed with a small hammer. And there must be *pompe à l'huile*, the flat cake made of olive-oil-enriched bread dough. These are served with *vin cuit*, a homemade sweet wine made by boiling grape juice to concentrate it and then topping it up with neutral spirits.

The *pompe à l'huile* has many points of gastronomic contact with other Christmas foods. In the village in the Var that my family frequents, it is usually transmuted to *fougasse*, which is normally sold by the baker in its savoury form, with cheese or particularly fat bits of bacon. In its sweet manifestation, also called *fouaces*, it can be made with orange-flower water, flavoured with anise, or, as in the Niçoise *fougassette*, with saffron and candied fruit.

The symbolism goes even further in some households, for the 13 desserts are set out on the table with the *santons*. These modelled clay idols have evolved from the figures of the *crèche*, the Christmas crib, St Francis's *presepio*. The Provençal figures, influenced by the Portuguese practice of adding realistic secular figures to those of the Holy Family, the Magi, shepherds and animals, are representatives of the workers, peasants, artisans and craftsmen of Provence. There is the fisherman and the woman fishmonger; the garlic-seller and the wild-mushroom gatherer; the shepherd in his smock, the baker in his whites and the peasant housewife in her Provençal print apron.

The *santons*, sometimes life-size, are now found in Christmas *crèches* in homes and in churches as well all over France, not just in Provence. How, we have to wonder, did these very profane images acquire the right to be displayed in sacred surroundings? In Sicily there is a group of very large, carved stone idols dedicated to the cult of Cybele, and dating from the 5th century or so BC. They are called the *Santoni*. It really does make one wonder.

One last matter. What should one drink with the Christmas dessert course? If, like us, you've chopped and changed and drunk several wines already, the dessert wine really has to be something to make any impact at all. It makes perfect sense at this point to go back to something fizzy (or to have something fizzy for the first time if you have had only still wine so far). Probably the best choice for this slot in the meal is a low-alcohol (which is a great merit at this point), peachy-sweet Moscato d'Asti. With its gentle mousse and gentle price, it's hard to beat – and goes equally well with Christmas pudding, or the snake, or ice cream, come to that.

Sauternes, or a Barsac, is a dearer alternative, but you need one with a lot of 'noble rot' or botrytis character to face up to Christmas pudding. Andrew Quady's California oddities, his orange muscat Essencia and his red Elysium, have what it takes to partner plum pudding, too. But a fortified wine has much to commend it, and this might be the time to experiment with Australian 'stickies', such as the coffee-coloured Galway Pipe or one of the several Brown Brothers' dessert wines. If you are having port, and drinking it with the cheese, why not carry on with the dessert? Or – my most original idea – try an old, sweet sherry. In my own cellar I have Valdespino Solera 1842 Oloroso Viejo Dulce, and three choices from Gonzales Byass: Amontillado del Duque, Apostoles Oloroso Abocado and Matusalem Oloroso Muy Viejo. At one time or another I have tasted them all, and I cannot think of anything they would marry with half as well as Christmas pudding.

FRANCES BISSELL'S CHRISTMAS PUDDING

Serves 8–10; fills a 1.75-litre (3-pint) pudding basin

230 g (8 oz, 4 loosely packed cups) fresh wholemeal breadcrumbs

230 g (8 oz, 2 cups) *each* of roughly chopped muscatel (black) raisins, sultanas (yellow raisins) and dried apricots

60 g (2 oz, ¾ cup) crumbled almond macaroons or amaretti

60 g (2 oz, ¾ cup) chopped almonds

60 g (2 oz, ½ cup) ground or flaked almonds

1 grated apple

1 Tbsp grated orange zest

1 tsp ground cinnamon

1 tsp ground mace

½ tsp ground cardamom

½ tsp ground cloves

½ tsp ground allspice

2 Tbsp orange marmalade or candied orange peel

juice of 1 orange

4 medium free-range eggs

6 Tbsp or 1 miniature bottle of Cognac

140 ml (5 fl oz, scant ⅔ cup) fortified muscat wine, port, marsala or rich *oloroso* sherry

Put all the dry ingredients in a large bowl and mix thoroughly. Put the marmalade, orange juice, eggs, brandy and wine in another large bowl, or in the blender or food processor, and beat until well blended and frothy. Pour the liquid over the dry ingredients. Mix until moist. Cover and let stand for a couple of hours at least and, if possible, overnight to let the spice flavours develop.

Oil or butter the pudding basin and spoon in the mixture. As it contains no raw flour, it will not expand very much during the cooking, so you can fill the basin to within 1.25 cm (½ in) of the rim. Take a square of greaseproof or waxed paper, oil or butter it, and tie it over the top of the basin with string.

Place the filled pudding basin in a saucepan, with a long triple-folded strip of foil under it and coming up both sides. This is to help you lift the boiling hot basin out of the saucepan once it is cooked. Pour in boiling water to go halfway up the pudding basin, cover the saucepan and bring it back to the boil. Then lower the heat and keep the water at a steady simmer so that the pudding steams for 5 hours. Keep the water level topped up with boiling water.

When the time is up, remove the pudding from the pan and allow it to cool completely before wrapping it, still in its basin, in fresh greaseproof paper plus a layer of foil. Store in a cool, dark place.

On Christmas Day, steam the pudding for a further two hours. Then decorate it with holly, warm some brandy or rum in a ladle and anoint the pudding with it. Remember to turn off the lights before you bring it into the dining room. We prefer to eat it with only a blob of *crème fraîche*. Brandy butter rather undoes the good of this pudding, which has no fat except for the egg yolks and only the sugar of the dried fruits and the tiny bit of marmalade.

HELGE RUBINSTEIN AND SHEILA BUSH'S CHRISTMAS PUDDING ICE

Ice cream made with some of the ingredients of Christmas pudding is a deliciously light alternative to the Real Thing, one that is much appreciated when the meal has been composed of several rich courses. I shouldn't recommend serving this ice cream in a blaze of brandy; but if there are only three or four guests, and if you are serving it in flameproof dishes, there would be no harm in warming some brandy or rum in a ladle, taking a match to it, and pouring just a little flaming alcohol over each serving. This dish bears a strong resemblance to what we used to call Nesselrode ice cream. The same ingredients were made into a syrupy sauce and poured over vanilla ice cream, or incorporated into an ice cream parfait.

Serves 4–6

175 g (6 oz, 1¾ cups) mixed dried and glacé fruits, such as currants, raisins, sultanas, orange and citron peel, marrons glacés, roughly chopped. You could make up part of the quantity with pecans, if you like them.

4 Tbsp light rum

300 ml (10 fl oz, 1¼ cup) single or light cream

5 egg yolks

140 g (5 oz, ½ cup) caster (fine) sugar

2 heaped Tbsp unsweetened chestnut purée (from a tin or a tube)

100 g (4 oz) Chocolate Menier or bittersweet chocolate

300 ml (10 fl oz, 1¼ cup) double or heavy cream, whipped until thick

Put the fruit to marinate and swell in the rum. Heat the single cream until almost boiling – when the surface trembles a little. Whisk the egg yolks with the sugar in a bowl, and pour the near-boiling cream over them, whisking constantly. Return the egg, sugar and cream mixture to the saucepan, and whisk over a very gentle heat until you have a thick custard. Be careful or you will have scrambled egg. If you don't trust your nerves, do this step in a *bain marie*, with a metal bowl suspended over, but not touching, the simmering water in the saucepan below.

When you're happy with the thickness of the mixture, whisk in the chestnut purée and then the chocolate, in small pieces. Stir until the chocolate is melted completely and the texture is smooth. Taste for sweetness. If the chocolate is particularly bitter, you might need a little more sugar. Leave to cool.

Now incorporate the plumped-up fruits and nuts (if used), and fold in the whipped cream.

If you like, you can freeze the ice in a pudding basin, and decorate it with a sprig of holly when you turn it out for serving. To do this, line the pudding basin in foil or fat-safe cling film. Pour in the mixture and freeze. If you can be bothered to give it a stir when it's half frozen, it will improve the texture marginally. Turn it out of the basin at least 1 hour before you mean to serve it. In fact, after a day you can turn it out, replace it in the freezer, and reclaim the pudding basin for another use.

Alternatively, you can freeze it in individual ramekins or soufflé dishes, or bung the whole lot into an electric ice-cream maker or sorbetière. But it should be allowed to 'ripen' for at least 1 hour in the fridge before you serve it.